JAZZ HEROES

JAZZ

HEROES

JOHN FORDHAM

A CHANNEL FOUR BOOK

C&B

First published in Great Britain in 1998 by
Collins & Brown Ltd.
London House
Great Eastern Wharf
Parkgate Road
London SW11 4NQ

Published in association with Channel Four Television Corporation
and based on the series produced by Uden Associates Limited
for Channel Four Television Corporation.

A CIP catalogue record of this book is available from the British Library

ISBN 1-85585-497-X (hb)
ISBN 1-85585-628-X (pb)

Editor: Corinne Asghar
Design Concept: David Fordham
Designer: Suzanne Megginson
Picture Research: Frances Abraham

Editorial Director: Sarah Hoggett
Art Director: Roger Bristow

Colour reproduction: Hong Kong Graphic and Printing Ltd.
Printed and bound in Great Britain by
Butler & Tanner Ltd, Frome and London

CONTENTS

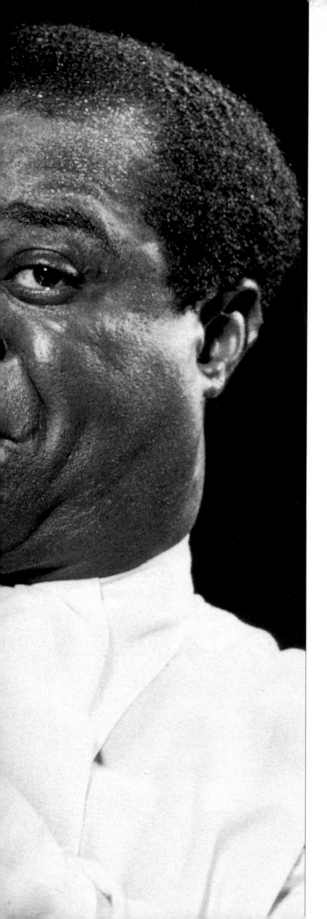

CHAPTER 1

THE STORY OF JAZZ

What *is* jazz?

Some very well-placed insiders have ducked that one. The popular sophistry goes: 'If you gotta ask, you'll never know'. Duke Ellington and Miles Davis, universally acclaimed jazz giants, tried to avoid using the word 'jazz' at all. The great pianist Ahmad Jamal, one of the few players Miles Davis ever quoted as an influence (and a man who grew up in Pittsburgh learning Mozart and Art Tatum side by side) prefers 'American classical music'.

Yet something generally called jazz has transformed music and dance all over the world in this century, and books, movies and everyday street-corner speech as well. It surfaces today in contemporary classical music, and in recent pop forms like 'acid jazz', in jazz samples reshuffled by ingenious dancefloor DJs, and it has echoes in rhythm-centred pop like '90s drum 'n' bass.

But if jazz is hard to pin down, it does have many identifying marks – although they may not all coincide in any single example of jazz, or sometimes be so wraithlike in their influence as to be barely detectable at all. Here are some of them – but for every one, there's a cautionary note. Jazz has been too fluid and mercurial, and still is, for its essence to be captured in a bottle permanently marked with any of the following ingredients.

You might begin by saying that jazz is an attitude to making music, or an alliance of ways of making music, in which at least some improvisation takes place. The cautionary note is that although some jazz performances are hardly written and prepared at all beforehand (although the ground rules will probably be tacitly agreed), some are extensively written and rehearsed. Great jazz has been made in both circumstances.

Jazz melody often has a distinctive feel. It frequently uses more imprecise pitching than European classical music, and often shares its intonation with the blues. Yet the jazz solo sound extends from trumpeter James 'Bubber' Miley's growl and use of the wah-wah, mute or Thelonious Monk's dissonances, to saxophonists Stan Getz or Paul Desmond's ethereal, violin-like purity.

Mostly, but not always, there is a steady underlying rhythmic pulse, sometimes called 'swing'. But unlike the unmissable, slamming backbeat of much dance-music or pop, the jazz pulse may seem more elusive and unpredictable, its accents asymmetrically scattered. Yet however rhythmically ambiguous it gets, most jazz reveals a sway, or undulation, or 'feel' or 'vibe' or 'groove' of some kind, which will often be detectable as an undertow to the loosest of performances. This feel is usually taken to be the most unmistakable echo of jazz music's African ancestry, and it's one of the most sensuous and communicative qualities of jazz.

Former slaves in the South, shortly after the American Civil War that brought emancipation. Much of the rhythmic drive and unorthodox intonation that gives jazz its unique flavour came with the slaves from Africa.

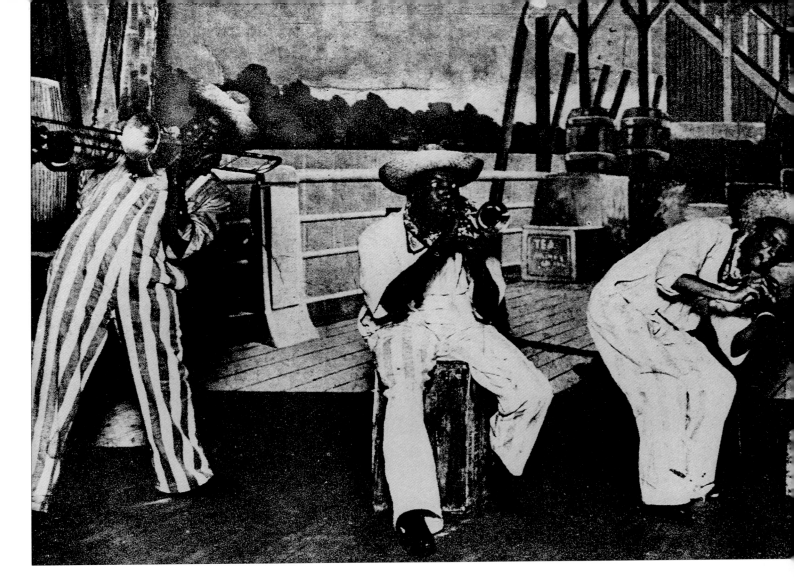

A New Orleans band of 1915. Jazz at this time was still largely a collective music of supportively interwoven lines, over marching rhythms and ragtime beats. Cornet or trumpet players took the lead.

Most importantly of all, the individual player calls the shots. Jazz musicians strive to cultivate an individual sound on their instruments, as unique as a signature or a smile – rather than the academically acceptable purity of tone and uniformity of method of much European art-music. Even today, when there are many more jazz colleges and jazz courses endorsing respectable methodologies, jazz players frequently continue to be self-taught.

So where did jazz begin?

It began with isolation, fear, stoicism, reminiscence, solidarity and hope. Ashantis, Yorubas, Dahomeans and Senegalese, four million of them by the middle of the 19th century, made up the slave population of North America when the outcome of the Civil War finally outlawed the practice. Their music crossed a variety of West African cultures, in which vocal and percussion music was dominant, scales and harmony were more intuitive and flexible, and the presence of spoken African languages dependent on pitch variation for meaning loaded subtle inflections of sound with rich implications.

Western missionaries to Africa had already begun a transformation in the continent's music by imposing the

'The liturgy of the Christian Church inevitably adapted to the traditional music of its new congregation.'

unfamiliar intervals of European hymns on traditional African tonalities, and out of this broth a unique resource evolved. It was a strange scale, in which the third and seventh tones were curiously flattened by comparison with the European tempered version, defying conventional notation. These distorted tones came to be known as 'blue notes'. They are a fundamental and recurring presence in jazz.

West Africans, giving music a vital lubricating role in all aspects of everyday social life and work, spurred slave-labour with song, and their masters encouraged it for its effect on productivity. And the church, finally acknowledging in Methodism that the Christian justification for slavery (namely that savages didn't have souls that needed to be saved) was incompatible with a doctrine of love, went out to embrace the slaves into the fold in a long campaign through the 19th century. African culture, however, was too strong to be overwhelmed. The liturgy of the Christian Church inevitably adapted to the traditional music of its new congregation as much as African music adapted to the hymn-books, and a rich new seam of ring-shouts (mutated from African circle-dances), camp songs, hymns and funeral chants entered the musical language of the New World. In gospel music today, this connection is still vividly audible.

Two worlds were mingling, and in some parts of the country they mixed more intimately than others. New Orleans, one of the most cosmopolitan cities in the Union, was just such a place.

In this seething seaport, many musics came together. Church music, African dance-music, French brass band soirée music and opera, black plantation music of the itinerant guitar-players and their defiant, confessional hybrid-form called 'the blues', an impassioned blend of church song and African lament. The African influence was also crossing the elegant, drawing-room culture of bourgeois Europe in the piano-dominated 'ragtime', a vivacious mixture of light classics and dance tunes which combined a steady, European pulse in one hand with a disrupted, offbeat, Africanised one in the other. 'Ragged time', appropriately, was the origin of the name. 'Syncopation' described the hitching of these unfamiliar rhythmic partners together.

In New Orleans, there was a voracious market-place for these new musics. The city's red-light district was sanctioned by local politician Alderman Sidney Story in 1898, and Storyville became part of jazz legend, its dives and honky-tonks providing work for hundreds of musicians. The city's Creole culture of educated blacks helped smooth the way for a schooled elegance and precision, particularly among clarinet players, to mingle with the raucousness of parade music and the fervour of church song and the blues. French brass-band and marching-music, crossed with the influence of African ritual dance recalled by former slaves in New Orleans' Congo Square, brought a new ensemble music to life.

Three principal lines were usually combined – cornet (trumpets were not yet widely used), trombone and clarinet. The cornet played the main melody, and then variations on it. The trombone lent depth to the sound, and marked the root notes of the chord changes. The clarinet – faster, more fluid and lighter – wove related melodies around them, and between the three, the constituent notes of the simple chord forms of early jazz (triads) could be played. But this was primarily a collective music - reflecting Southern black working and social life, and the virtual absence, so far, of improvisers skilled enough to extemporise for long on their own.

The rhythm of this music was repetitive, closer to a march-beat than to syncopation, but engaging. Its leading practitioners in New Orleans, bandleaders Charles 'Buddy' Bolden, Bunk Johnson and Freddie

Keppard, began to forge a vibrant, jostling music of unusual tonality and vocalised sounds close to the blues. By 1913, the music was beginning to be herded under the umbrella of 'jass', a word for sexual intercourse according to Sidney Bechet, and appropriately associated with this louche and sensuous music's accompaniment to the bumps, grinds and slow drags of the bordellos.

As jass caught on, some whites noticed. Papa Jack Laine was a white bandleader in New Orleans, and it was his trumpeter Nick LaRocca who brought a jazz band to New York, an eastern city that had hardly heard of the new musical form. The Original Dixieland Jass Band opened at Reisenweber's Restaurant on Columbus Circle in 1917, was an instant hit, cut the first ever jazz records, and launched The Jazz Age.

The ODJB had a raw exuberance that conveyed some of the flavour of New Orleans jazz, but it wasn't the real

The King Oliver Creole Band of 1923 that really started it all. From left: Johnny Dodds (clarinet), Baby Dodds (drums), Honore Dutrey (trombone), Louis Armstrong (cornet), Joe 'King' Oliver (cornet), Lil Hardin (piano), Bill Johnson (banjo). Oliver's band was a taut, bluesy outfit, but Armstrong shot out of it like a comet.

The great Duke Ellington. They called Edward Kennedy Ellington 'Duke' because he was so dapper and elegant. But there was nothing dapper about his music, which combined the sinewy energy and spontaneity of jazz with classical music's depth of texture.

thing. The band led by New Orleans cornettist Joe 'King' Oliver, however, certainly was. It still exhibited the static rhythms and cramped ensemble feel of the prototype jazz bands, but the sound of the group was hotter and more passionate, the individual voices (though still devoted primarily to a collective music) were more distinctive, notably the blues-steeped Johnny Dodds on clarinet.

With the eventual closing of Storyville in 1917 and the rapid expansion of heavy industry in the North, blacks migrated from the farms to the factories, and the musicians went too. Some performers with jazz potential went on the road with the popular minstrel shows and tent shows, sometimes demeaning work for a black artist,

but work nonetheless. Many played the riverboats as they plied their way up and down the Mississippi towards the north. Jazz was spreading fast.

King Oliver went to Chicago in 1918 to work in the black South Side clubs, formed his own band two years later, and a new public (of enthusiastic young whites, as well as blacks) began to thrill to the sound. And then, King Oliver brought Louis Daniel Armstrong to Chicago.

Armstrong was a brass-playing prodigy, raised in the New Orleans ghetto, musically educated in the streets and in a children's home, singing four-part harmony for dimes. His harmonic intuitions were extraordinary, his spontaneous counter-melodies against King Oliver's lead revolutionised the jazz front line overnight, and his technique left all his contemporaries, even Oliver himself, at the start line. Armstrong's genius unleashed virtuoso jazz improvising, displacing notes so they no longer sat routinely on top of the beat, and varying accents and dynamics to impart the qualities of speech – and when he recorded with his own *Hot Five* and *Hot Seven* bands in a period of explosive creativity between 1925 and 1928, some of the great classics of jazz music were captured.

As Charlie Parker was to do 20 years later, Armstrong's vision, clarity and attack influenced musicians on all instruments, and composers and arrangers too. He had no serious rivals as a brass improvisor during the 1920s – save one. Leon 'Bix' Beiderbecke, the Iowa-born son of German immigrants, who had heard Armstrong in the riverboat bands, was the first great white jazz artist. His phrasing was as distinctive as Armstrong's but his sound was stately and pure-toned, and in his delicacy and his drawing on ideas from classical composers, notably Debussy, some consider him to be an early forerunner of bebop and its 'cool' style offspring of two decades later.

Alcoholism and pneumonia killed Beiderbecke at 28 in 1931, before he had achieved much public appreciation. But his influence on white musicians in Chicago helped to found a distinct style, based on New Orleans music but with extended solos, and featuring musicians who were to become jazz celebrities, including clarinettist Benny Goodman and drummer Gene Krupa.

Jelly Roll Morton was another crucial creator of early jazz. A gifted pianist with a gargantuan ego who had begun his career in the New Orleans brothels around 1902 (and varied it with episodes of pimping, gambling and pool-hustling), he later claimed he had created jazz single-handed. He hadn't but he certainly did fuse a wide variety of local idioms, including ragtime, blues, minstrel music, hymns and Hispanic styles. And with the Red Hot Peppers in Chicago in 1926-7 he achieved a balance of improvisation and composition (and a remarkable empathy of creative piano accompaniment), using this rich palette of references, that was unique in the jazz of the day. Like Armstrong's Hot bands, Morton's pioneering work was fortunately also caught by the fast-developing recording technology of the day, and from 1925 onward was vastly improved in audibility by the development of the electric microphone.

But it was Louis Armstrong's call that was heard the loudest and clearest. Even the elegant dance-bands back east, playing a more urbane arranged music for a

> 'Armstrong's genius unleashed virtuoso jazz improvising . . .varying accents and dynamics to impart the qualities of speech.'

sophisticated clientele, heard it and sent out for 'hot' trumpet players, though between 1921 and 1926 a kind of light classical music with a few tastefully distributed splashes of jazz colour ('symphonic jazz') was more popular with white audiences, and bandleader Paul Whiteman was briefly and inappropriately dubbed 'The King of Jazz' on the strength of it.

It wasn't long before a hotter flavour of jazz seasoned with New Orleans spice began to win the edge. It touched Edward Kennedy 'Duke' Ellington, the piano-playing son of a Washington butler who intended his son to be a painter, who had come to New York with a band of friends in 1923. Ellington and his Washingtonians' genteel music didn't fire until Sidney Bechet (briefly) and a wild New Orleans trumpeter, James 'Bubber' Miley joined in.

It touched Fletcher Henderson, a classically-trained and university-educated pianist originally destined to be a chemist, but who found that a mixture of racism and a diffident temperament blocked his route to a middle-class career. Henderson turned to music instead, and formed a band in New York in 1923, originally closer to symphonic jazz than New Orleans. But for a Harlem booking at the Roseland Ballroom the next year, Henderson realised his audience was ready for something with a little more bite.

Henderson brought Louis Armstrong to New York to be his hot soloist, and (along with musical director Don Redman) began to develop a new ensemble sound. Louis Armstrong's audacity of improvised phrasing, soaring away from the apparently inexorable grip of the New Orleans two-beat rhythm and its steady, predictable syncopation, was so bold a departure that composers

'Bechet was remarkable, with a skill and bounding imagination that almost rivalled Armstrong's.'

were as drawn to it as soloists were – so Redman and Henderson began writing ensemble parts that sounded like fragments of Armstrong solos.

Symphonic jazz had also provided one technique with considerable potential (Paul Whiteman's arrangers Ferde Grofe and Bill Challis had explored it), that of setting the brass and reed sections in creative tension with each other. The development opened up a much more powerful role for the saxophone, previously consigned to risible chicken-clucking effects in vaudeville shows, or swooning violin-mimicry in dance bands.

Before the mid-1920s, the only undisputed jazz-sax hero was the New Orleans musician Sidney Bechet, who had switched from clarinet to the soprano saxophone in 1919 and produced a music of mercurial and passionate intensity with it. Bechet was so remarkable, with a skill and bounding imagination that almost rivalled Armstrong's, that even classical musicians were astonished. When Bechet was in Europe with the Southern Syncopators, a black symphonic band with limited use for jazz, the Swiss conductor Ernest Ansermet published an ecstatic article in praise of him, the first

prominent public endorsement of jazz by a formal musician. Ansermet unequivocally welcomed Bechet as 'an artist of genius'.

Saxophonists began to emerge in Bechet's wake and to fill the spaces opening in the new jazz bands. Boston altoist Johnny Hodges had worked with Bechet and been profoundly influenced by his sound, an impact that was to have much wider significance when Hodges joined Duke Ellington in 1928. The Fletcher Henderson Orchestra hired Coleman Hawkins, a schooled musician who had worked in tent shows and blues groups. Hawkins' (the original liberator of the tenor saxophone from its side-show origins) cultured phrasing, big sound and narrative drive, had been inspired by Armstrong's trumpet, and by the prodigious pianist Art Tatum.

Tatum represented an approach to improvisation that gained prominence as jazz evolved. And his background, like Thomas 'Fats' Waller's, went back to the ragtime-based 'stride school' of the early years. A piano prodigy from Toledo with a technique the equal of a classical virtuoso, Tatum began to use a different approach to improvising to Armstrong's melodic variations on the tune, using the harmonic structures of songs as the basis for improvising, a departure that was to change jazz.

The novelist Scott Fitzgerald heralded the 1920s as 'The Jazz Age', and the clamorous vivacity of the new

Benny Goodman, here playing the Waldorf Astoria in 1938, was dubbed 'The King of Swing'. When the Swing craze took hold in the 1930s it was the pop music of its day.

shows and travelling vaudeville acts had constituted much of the itinerant life of the entertainment business before, now it was jazz bands, playing one-nighters all over the country in ever-increasing numbers.

The jazz phenomenon coincided with, and may have partly fuelled, a briefly incandescent social upheaval centred on New York known as the 'Harlem Renaissance'. This was an opening up of recognition for black American music, literature, art and history. Fashionable white society embarked on a fascinated tourism of the Harlem night-spots and as the thriving mob-run, illicit-alcohol nightlife of rival jazz capital

music invaded the ballrooms, nightclubs, dives, bars and even concert halls. Paul Whiteman even commissioned George Gershwin to premiere 'Rhapsody in Blue' at New York's Aeolian Hall in 1924. And it wasn't just restricted to New York, however much of a jazz capital the city became toward the end of the 1920s. Where the tent

Chicago declined with the ending of Prohibition, New York's eclecticism turned it into the third hub of jazz.

A revitalised culture nurtured jazz, but as a growing audience grew more familiar with it and the methods of jazz musicians more sophisticated, both the blues and New Orleans traditions began to rapidly date. The process was accelerated by the Wall Street Crash of 1929, and the subsequent economic depression. The blues, which was an intimate partner of New Orleans jazz and had been a popular idiom with black audiences

particularly (the great singer Bessie Smith's success was based on it) began to seem the wrong music for the mood. Black buying power, never bullish, weakened further with unemployment, and the segregated 'race records' industry went down with it.

But if the loose change in the public's pockets grew lighter, hard times redoubled its desire for a good time, to forget disaster, to savour vivid moments, to dance. So, despite the slump, musicians still worked. The 'Austin High School Gang' of creative white musicians including

Jazz moved fast, from folk-art to modern art in two decades. This is Minton's Playhouse in the early 1940s, the original laboratory for bebop experimentation. From left, Thelonious Monk, trumpeters Howard McGhee and Roy Eldridge and bandleader Teddy Hill.

clarinet virtuoso Benny Goodman and trumpeter Jimmy McPartland, went hungry and scuffled for jobs, but they were young and believed in better times. When the New Deal and an economic upturn came, they were ready. Swing was the overture of the New Deal – a loud, fast, jubilant, confident, highly organised music that used bigger ensembles, charismatic soloists, showbiz presentation and a smoother and more flowing feel to the beat. The two-beat 'boom-chick' of early jazz was gone.

White bands led by Benny Goodman, the Dorsey Brothers, and trombonist Glenn Miller got big, and so did black ones like the exciting Kansas-based Count Basie Orchestra, Jimmie Lunceford's band and, of course, Duke Ellington. Benny Goodman went from comparative obscurity as a gifted, hard-working but rather derivative mix of New Orleans and classical influences, to a nationwide celebrity almost overnight (aided by the growth of coast-to-coast radio) and eventually became dubbed 'The King of Swing'. Great instrumental soloists matured, like saxophonists Coleman Hawkins, the poetic, ethereal Lester Young, the romantic Ben Webster and Johnny Hodges (with Duke Ellington), fiery trumpeters Roy Eldridge and Buck Clayton. There was also a new breed of singer, a true jazz improviser. Although the subtle and bluesy Billie Holiday was more suited to intimate surroundings than big bands, Ella Fitzgerald was a dynamic orchestral vocalist, at times imitating the sound of the other instruments in the wordless singing style Louis Armstrong had made popular, called 'scat'.

Duke Ellington's Orchestra was as exciting an outfit in the ballrooms as any big 1930s swing ensemble, but Ellington took jazz materials to previously unimagined heights. Ellington and his musicians frequently evolved new pieces by improvisational experimentation, and

though the leader's vision (and that of his gifted assistant Billy Strayhorn) drew all the strands of the band into a single entity, such early jazz classics such as 'Creole Love Call', 'Mood Indigo' and 'Sophisticated Lady' were born out of an open manner of composition that had no parallel in formal notated music.

But Ellington's method did resemble more formal music in its variations of pace and dynamics and the subtlety of its textures, although the similarity ended with the sustained eloquence of the improvisers and the intensity of the band's rhythmic drive when it chose to turn it on. Other fine orchestras opted for more direct methods, closer to boogie-woogie, stride piano and the blues – notably Count Basie's orchestra, which

Tenor saxophonist Coleman Hawkins. Hawkins came up with the swing bands, perfecting an expressively logical technique for the tenor that thousands copied. Swing tenorists everywhere wanted to take him on, but he floored all the opposition except Lester Young.

'Early jazz classics such as "Creole Love Call" and "Mood Indigo" were born out of an open manner of composition that had no parallel in formal notated music.'

Swing was the dominant music in World War II, and captain Glen Miller (above) led one of the most commercially successful of all. The big bands were hit hard by recruitment in the war years, and postwar economics made it harder for them to recover. Yet Miller had special responsibility for co-ordinating military entertainment. He disappeared on a flight in 1944.

favoured repeated, steadily punching chordal shouts behind the soloists, a technique that was known as 'the riff'. Benny Goodman's band mixed this with a smoothed-out New Orleans sound, and at the height of his fame Goodman began mixing black jazz stars (guitarist Charlie Christian, vibraphonist Lionel Hampton, pianist Teddy Wilson) into his largely white outfit, a controversial move at the time that eventually paid him dividends.

At the height of Swing's success, as World War II loomed, a 20th-century equation applied – innovation plus runaway success equals a formula. The bigger Swing became, the more the public wanted its practitioners to repeat themselves. But jazz, a music centred on the individual and on spontaneity and rapid change, could not contain such a paradox for long.

Swing was built for dancing, and its groove was four beats to the bar, with an emphasis on the first and third, heavily flagged by the bass drum. Some younger musicians were bored with that feeling, and drummers such as Kenny Clarke (working with the Teddy Hill swing band) began to change it around. In 1940, Clarke was hired to book a house band for a Harlem club called Minton's Playhouse. It was a popular haunt for musicians, particularly for after-hours relaxation and informal jam sessions. Clarke found a unconventional young stride and gospel pianist with a quirky harmonic ear called Thelonious Monk. John Birks 'Dizzy' Gillespie, a musically sophisticated and explosively agile trumpeter came too, as did Benny Goodman's star guitarist Charlie Christian. Gillespie, Christian and others were using the materials of their regular work in the swing orchestras as the basis for a new music - stacking the simpler chords of standard songs with extra notes (minor 7ths were popular, rarely used in jazz before but common in the work of formal composers including Debussy). It was partly a challenge, partly a way of avoiding paying royalties on the originals, and introducing dissonances, greatly accelerated intensity and speed of delivery, and strange resolutions that sometimes seemed to leave tunes hanging in space.

Of all these musicians, the most charismatic and instinctively innovative (as Louis Armstrong had been before him) was Charlie Parker, the young Kansas City alto saxophonist. Raised by a doting mother, driven by a musical vision that possessed him, Parker had begun by

Charlie Parker (centre), flanked by bassist Tommy Potter and trumpeter Miles Davis. Parker blew away the cosy sentimentality and song-like tune structures of swing as if its formidable resources were paper-thin. Chaotic in personal habits and short-lived, Parker nevertheless revolutionised jazz vocabulary in the style called bebop.

extensively copying the phrasing of Kansas sax hero Lester Young, particularly in Young's long, legato lines and logical melodic development. Parker inadvertently taught himself to play in all keys (unaware that no jazz musicians did), and began to perceive jazz melody lines in a new way, using the upper notes of more complex chords (9ths, 11ths and 13ths), not just for brief effects, as the swing players had done, but as the raw material for improvised solos. It imparted such an unexpected quality at first that some swing stars and critics dismissed it as no longer jazz at all. Yet Parker was a jazz musician in every raw nerve, and the most haunting blues instrumentalist to come to jazz since Louis Armstrong.

The new idiom was first called 'rebop' and then 'bebop', after its characteristically disruptive rhythmic feel. It shook jazz out of swing's complacency, but it wasn't without formulae of its own – constant intensity and the obligation to memorise and juggle countless fragments of scales and phrasing to be able to sustain the pace in an improvising situation.

Some bop musicians considered these could lead to the same kind of formulaic repetition that had driven them away from swing in the first place. Trumpeter Miles Davis, who had lionised Charlie Parker and played in his quintet, but never paralleled his method in the way Dizzy Gillespie did, was one of these. Davis had a softer and more fragile sound than Gillespie, and in the 1940s a less commanding technique, but he was intrigued by a development in larger-group jazz that played to his strengths. Working with a group of New York arrangers and performers including saxophonists Gerry Mulligan and Lee Konitz, and Canadian arranger Gil Evans, Davis sought a fusion of jazz improvisation and formal composition that echoed the relationship of improvisation to 'symphonic jazz' of twenty years before, and also Bix Beiderbecke's Debussyan musings. But this kind of jazz-chamber music was inflected with a very different melodic and rhythmic feel, because its players were of Charlie Parker's generation and feeling for jazz had been turned around by him, even if the experiment was a counterbalance to Parker's kind of bop.

The Miles Davis Nonet that played the Birth of the Cool repertoire hardly performed live, although it did record. But the restrained, oblique cool style developed some fruitful variations, and the most accessible manifestations of it even made the pop charts in the early 1950s in the hands of baritone saxophonist Gerry Mulligan and a charismatic young white trumpeter, strongly influenced by Miles Davis, called Chet Baker. Baker and Mulligan developed a quietly garrulous, counter-melodic, conversational music of considerable freedom of line, because the band used no piano to anchor it to the harmony. It was a pianist however, who was the most influential guru to the 'Cool School' of musicians – the scholarly, uncompromising blind Chicago pianist Lennie Tristano, who eschewed busy drumming as a distraction and wide dynamic changes and emphatic climaxes as pandering to populism. Brilliant saxophonists Lee Konitz and Warne Marsh studied with Tristano, pursuing the priority of melodic variation over long lines above all else.

In 1955 Charlie Parker died at the age of 34 in New York, burned out by drug abuse and self neglect, and the jazz world was stunned by the loss. In his short lifetime the saxophonist had wrestled the steering wheel of jazz development away from the Swing players to pilot into the postwar world, a more ironic,

'The bigger Swing became, the more the public wanted its practitioners to repeat themselves.'

'... Parker was a jazz
musician in every raw nerve
and the most haunting
blues instrumentalist
to come to jazz since
Louis Armstrong.'

Pianist Lennie Tristano in the 1950s. A
fastidious, complex and demanding
musician and teacher, Tristano disliked
the grandstanding of some jazz
approaches and wanted his music quiet,
undemonstrative and concentrated
rigorously on the melody lines.

unsentimental and rigorous music yet with the heat and
passion of the early pioneers and the mathematical
elegance of Bach. Parker's career was hampered by drugs
and alcohol in his last years, but his recordings with
bands including Dizzy Gillespie and later Miles Davis in
the mid 1940s became landmarks to rival the Hot Fives
and Sevens. Davis himself, once asked to explain jazz
evolution, said it could be related in four words: Louis
Armstrong, Charlie Parker.

Postwar jazz was dominated by Parker's example, but
Duke Ellington and Thelonious Monk went their own
way. Ellington had run one of his finest ensembles in the
1940s, evolving beyond the decline of swing. Monk too,
had begun a run of spikily individualistic composing and
playing that after his death led to pieces like 'Round
Midnight', 'Rhythm-a-ning' and 'Evidence' entering even
the repertoire of classical pianists seeking to represent
the great compositions of the 20th century.

Bebop spawned a sibling known as 'hard bop' in the
1950s and early 1960s, which emphasised blues and
gospel themes, and very extended solos. Its principal
exponents were drummers Max Roach and Art Blakey,
pianist Horace Silver, trumpeters Lee Morgan and
Clifford Brown and saxophonists Lou Donaldson, Hank
Mobley, Sonny Rollins and John Coltrane. The invention
of the long-playing microgroove record made the idiom's
extended solos available outside of a live performance,
and with hard bop mutations towards pop and soul

THE STORY
OF JAZZ

music (Horace Silver coined a lasting musical label with his tune 'Opus De Funk'), jazz attempted to take on the genre that was forcing it offstage with younger audiences in the 1950s – rock'n'roll. Ironically rock'n'roll had itself sprung from a hectic, repetitive variation on swing called 'jump', with infusions of country-music and blues.

Trumpeter Miles Davis turned out to be one of the most restless experimenters and transformers in jazz history. Although he led a brilliant hard bop band in the mid-1950s, with an fearsome saxophone discovery in John Coltrane, he was as suspicious of long-term potential of

improvising over song-form chords as he had been in the 'Birth of the Cool' period, and began to explore modes, or cycles of scales, instead – a method already explored and documented by a former bop drummer turned brilliant experimental bandleader, George Russell in the book 'The Lydian Chromatic Concept of Tonal Organisation'. Modalism resulted in a more relaxed, open, melodically loose kind of jazz, and with 'Kind of Blue', Davis recorded his most famous and influential exploration of the method, in the company of John Coltrane, pianists Wynton Kelly and Bill Evans, and others.

Sonny Rollins (left) is a colossus of saxophone improvisation and is still playing today. Rollins was influenced by Charlie Parker's complexity, but also liked Coleman Hawkins' big sound and Lester Young's poetic whimsicality.

Both Rollins and drummer Art Blakey (below) came up on the wave of 1950s 'hard bop', an extended bop style of complexity, high energy, blues and gritty attack. Blakey's cymbal beat was like a river in full flow.

The inbuilt contradiction of bebop – that it was an improviser's music of very inflexible harmonic rules – affected Davis, Coltrane and many other adventurous musicians at the beginning of the 1960s. The first two expressed their desire for change in characteristically different ways. Davis wanted to play less and use space and contrast. Coltrane wanted to play as much as possible, to create the illusion of more than one saxophonist's line, and intensify his music so that individual notes seemed to blur into a 'sheet of sound'.

Miles Davis and John Coltrane became models for their jazz generation and the ones that followed. And although they were further to the music's margins, Texas-born saxophonist Ornette Coleman, and classically-trained piano virtuoso Cecil Taylor did too, pointing the way towards methods of thematic improvisation that abandoned chords altogether. These

Saxophonist Ornette Coleman in 1969. Coleman was one of the most controversial jazz figures of the 1950s and 1960s. Abandoning the chords of songs, Coleman improvised without arranged structures. But although his music at first sounded chaotic to some, his place as an improviser has been confirmed by time.

changes led to the controversial 'free-music' scene of the 1960s, an unflinching revolution with a powerful input from radical black American musicians, paralleling the civil-rights movement, a growing liberalisation of personal politics alongside the celebration of collective and communal endeavour, and uninhibited artistic expressionism generally. John Coltrane became a symbol of artistic and spiritual liberation for many young listeners, his striving, wailing saxophone appealing to much the same audience as was entranced by rock star Jimi Hendrix's guitar.

Free music left improvisers with no defences, and listeners with few clues. In its most extreme forms it left no convenient themes to hide behind, or grooves to coast on, and the success of a performance was down to the ingenuity of the artist alone. But if the treatment for

bebop's rigidities sometimes killed the patient, free music also recaptured some of jazz's earliest expressionist impulses. Many jazz stars were affected by it, even if they didn't adopt it wholesale, including Sonny Rollins and the ever-vigilant Miles Davis.

Miles Davis died in 1991, but spent the last 20 years of his productive musical life leading jazz-funk bands that veered between black pop and the almost abstract - many young jazz performers today move comfortably between the rhythmic feel and melodic shapes of what were formerly thought of as incompatible idioms because of him. Like Pat Metheny, a guitarist from the midwest whose style was forged from a blend of the bop guitar virtuoso Wes Montgomery's smooth eloquence and the clang of country and rock guitarists. Pianist Keith Jarrett has also won a similar audience to Metheny for his

'Miles Davis and John
Coltrane became models
for their jazz generation
and the ones that
followed.'

bands emerged – Mike Westbrook, Loose Tubes, South
Africa's Brotherhood of Breath. In 1996 the English Arts
Council , usually a tentative defender of jazz compared to
classical music and opera, formally declared:

'Jazz music has completed the journey from rough-
hewn folk art to a sophisticated creative vehicle in
barely 90 years, paralleling the progression of
European classical music across five centuries . . . in
many ways, it can claim the title 'the art music of the
twentieth century.'

And so, as an open-structured music that has encouraged
the individual spirit both to rise above circumstance,
expectation and caution, and yet intimately coexist with
others, the great story of jazz in the 20th century has had
many heroes. This books is principally about the postwar
jazz world, and its six key heroes – chosen because for
the most part their stories have not been told before as
frequently as those of Charlie Parker or Miles Davis –
contributed hugely to jazz. But of course compelling
arguments could be made for six different ones, or six
more, or a score more. And since jazz has been a rallying
call for 'ordinary' people to be extraordinary, it could as
easily include the thousands of local heroes on an
inspired night, or an inspired hour, or just one inspired
song playing a tenor sax in the bar around the corner. But
if there are grounds for dissenting opinion on who is
entitled to be considered a jazz hero that history will not
forget, there is almost certainly consensus on one issue –
to qualify, none of the candidates should have left the
music as they found it. I hope the fascinating life stories
of these six great jazz artists, and the invaluable
contributions of those who knew them or were inspired
by them, do something to convey that, and the flavour of
this wonderful music of our time.

romantic yet wilful improvising, and bridging of classical
music and jazz, and he's loved by jazz and non-jazz
listeners alike. In recent years, and in response both to
free music and to Miles Davis' electric funk, a purist neo-
classical movement has sprung up too, devoted to the
acoustic, bop and modal-driven jazz of the 1950s and
1960s, and dominated by a young New Orleans trumpet
virtuoso, Wynton Marsalis.

The jazz message has now travelled all over the world,
to be reshaped by regional cultures, and to reshape them
in turn. In 1990, when Wynton Marsalis' career was on a
roll, *Time* magazine put him on its cover – one of a
handful of times that this paper had given a jazz musician
such endorsement. The cover line welcomed 'The New
Jazz Age'. Neo-classicism, through its neglect of jazz's
characteristic urge to innovate, put neglected older
talents back on the map like the great Rollins, influential
saxophonist Joe Henderson, and Rollins himself became
a cult figure, playing to ecstatic crowds of all ages
everywhere. Mike Brecker showed what could still
be done with Coltrane's pre-free style, and the wilder
shores of free sounds, previously so controversial, even
entered the mainstream. Coltrane's voice was heard in
an emerging international group of new jazz heroes –
John Surman, Evan Parker, Andy Sheppard and
Courtney Pine in Britain, the evocative Jan Garbarek in
Norway. Following Ellington and his avant-garde
disciple Charles Mingus, wonderful, free-flowing big

CHAPTER

2

DIZZY
GILLESPIE

'Dizzy's heart beat on one
beat, and Charlie Parker's
heart beat on the next beat,
that's how close they were . . .
the way they played together
sounded like one person.'

JOHN FADDIS — TRUMPETER

dressing rooms and hotels, you could be there on a night when his scorching high notes, sly, cajoling half-valve effects and headlong runs would seem to roll back the years. That night, at London's Festival Hall, his United Nations orchestra of Americans, Cubans, Puerto Ricans and Brazilians mixed delicacy and fireworks with ferocious enthusiam. Soaring chords dropped to soft accompaniments to Gillespie's inimitable late-career trumpet style. Sidelong mutterings and fitful double-tempo spurts spiralled off into turbine-like squeals and low, rumbling reverberations as if from a trombone. The bandleader's Alfred Hitchcock waddle to the microphone, with its atmosphere of menace and avuncular reassurance, was almost as central to the show as the peremptory summons of his horn.

Almost three and a half years later, in January 1993, Dizzy Gillespie died at his home in Englewood, New Jersey, and the world showered his memory with countless tributes. Jon Faddis, the trumpeter Gillespie called his 'musical son', says:

'even at that point, where he had cancer, he could still put it together. . . He was tired, but he wouldn't take a rest. I think he felt that if he put the horn down, that was almost putting his life down – laying down, not being able to live.'

'I've got to the age now where I read the obituary columns to see if I'm in.'

DIZZY GILLESPIE

IN LONDON, ONE MAY AFTERNOON in 1989, the trumpeter Dizzy Gillespie, one of jazz music's most original voices and one of its most celebrated clowns, was in exuberant form. It concealed the punishing city-a-night concert schedule he was facing. 'Phineas Newborn's dead' Gillespie declared. 'Read it in the *Herald Tribune*. I've got to the age now where I read the obituary columns to see if I'm in.' This wasn't a new gag, but Gillespie's charisma made it sound fresh. He did the same with the most routine pieces of music breathing new life into everything he touched.

Gillespie was 71 at this time, and mostly still playing like the master he had been for over fifty years. And although the performances late in Gillespie's career could occasionally be automatic and reflexive, as one might expect of any septuagenarian living in aeroplanes,

Dizzy on 52nd Street, New York. 'The Street' was the world hub of modern jazz in the '40s, with dozens of clubs, featuring the best in the business, side by side.

The remarkable John Birks 'Dizzy' Gillespie was a founder of modern jazz and a leading architect of its acceptance as one of the century's most illuminating and serious musical developments. He juggled artistry and showmanship, and was a stunning improviser, adventurous composer, and, not least, a symbol of optimism for racial harmony. A research medic even wrote a treatise on the famous 'Gillespie pouches' after seeing a picture of his extraordinary ballooning cheeks – a physiognomic act that ought to have been more than flesh and blood could stand, and which set orthodox trumpet teachers wringing their hands in despair.

The world outside jazz had come to realise that Dizzy Gillespie was a phenomenon to be cherished, however eccentric he might seem. In 1976, the Smithsonian Institution's Division of Performing Arts issued a two-record retrospective called 'The Development of an American Artist'. The producer and critic Martin Williams wrote: 'John Birks "Dizzy" Gillespie is a great figure in American music, in world music, and perhaps the greatest living musical innovator we have.'

Gillespie is now regarded as a genius who changed the course of jazz forever, and behind the facade of manic anarchism and showbiz bravura, was one of the sharpest minds in 20th-century music.

John Birks Gillespie was born, the youngest of nine children, in Cheraw, South Carolina on 21 October 1917, three months after the Original Dixieland Jass Band cut the first jazz records. His father was a bricklayer, but also a weekend bandleader, and the house was full of musical instruments. Gillespie's parents were Methodists, but he used to sneak off to the Sanctified Church on Sundays, fascinated, as he later said, by the way that 'music could transport people spiritually'. Gillespie Senior died when his youngest son was 10 years old. The young

John Birks was already developing an interest in the piano, and around 1928 he took up the trombone – but his true voice was yet to emerge.

He also practised on a neighbour's trumpet, and soon joined a marching band. Gillespie later recalled that the band only played in B flat, so when he showed up for an audition with a bandleader who wanted to play in C, he was mortified to discover he couldn't play at all.

THE
TRUMPET

UNTIL THE 1930S, the trumpet was the most familiar jazz symbol. Its penetrating attack and gleaming tone had much the same compelling effect in jazz as the various ancestors of the instrument had in military bands, on royal occasions and in religious imagery for centuries. An instrument that requires a great deal of sensitive input from the player to compensate for its structural peculiarities, the trumpet suited the idiosyncratic methods of jazz musicians.

The term 'trumpet' can refer to any lip-vibrated instrument, usually constructed from brass. The technique puts considerable strain on the technique and facial musculature of players, because the trumpet is an instrument with no internal reed – the 'reeds' are the lips of the performers, shaped in constantly changing ways to alter the pitch, and vibrated by carefully controlled breathing techniques.

The basic concept of today's trumpet goes back to the Middle Ages, but the valve system was added around 1815. Before that, the available notes on the 'natural' instrument were only what the trumpeter could form with the shape of the lips and mouth, or embouchure. Adding valves extended the length of the trumpet's tubing, and allowed different lengths to be selected by opening and closing the appropriate valves. This extended the available notes.

Demobilisation after the American Civil War increased the availability of cheap trumpets in the Southlands, which contributed to the instrument's widespread availability for dance and parade bands. Once adopted by many self-taught and improvising players, trumpet techniques changed fast. In jazz-playing, the upper register of the instrument has been considerably extended by embouchure and breathing methods alone – to the extent that high notes played by Dizzy Gillespie's early model Roy Eldridge, for instance, hit registers no conventional trumpeter believed possible.

Jazz trumpeters have also managed to mimic some of the sounds of the human voice by the use of growling and trilling effects, humming and blowing simultaneously, half-depressing the valves to produce slurred or imprecise notes, and by the use of a variety of mutes, to partially close the bell and produce an oblique, reticent sound.

The B-flat trumpet, the dominant brass instrument in jazz since it replaced the cornet in the late 1920s. The long tubing is folded for compactness, and the valves alter the air column by subdividing it into sections of varying lengths. After the mid 1950s, Dizzy Gillespie used a trumpet of his own (accidental) design with an angled bell.

Jitterbugging in Harlem. The dance halls were the homes of the swing bands – and swing was where Gillespie got started.

But musical life quickly improved. At 15, Gillespie won a scholarship to the Laurinburg Institute in North Carolina, having finally buckled down to formal trombone studies. He also heard the music of the bands touring the Southlands, and would occasionally sit in. But Gillespie's exposure to the most exciting bands of the swing era came about as a result of his mother's decision to move to Philadelphia in 1935. This industrial seaport, with its broad ethnic mix and rich cultural life, was to be almost as significant in the development of jazz and blues in the United States as New York, Chicago or New Orleans.

The brother of his French teacher at Laurinberg was swing-band leader Jimmie Lunceford's pianist, and the connection provided Gillespie with contacts among Lunceford's star players. Around the same time he heard the great Louis Armstrong, but although Gillespie recognised Armstrong's genius, Louis' sound belonged to an era that was already regarded with nostalgia by some. The music he heard in his head was more complex in structure, less lyrical. It was the future.

Dizzy's first role model Roy Eldridge (right) gets on down with saxophonist Flip Phillips (left) on the kind of *Jazz At The Philharmonic* roadshow where popping high notes brought the house down.

At 18, Gillespie joined Frankie Fairfax's big band in Philadelphia, around which time he acquired the 'Dizzy' nickname, reportedly for showing up for the job with his precious trumpet in a paper bag. His reputation for 'dizziness' grew over the coming years, through various antics with headgear, clothing and onstage furniture. However, although much of this was simply waywardness, it was also a symptom of his oppositional will. If a bandleader told Gillespie to take his feet off the chair, he'd put them on the music stand, and defend himself by saying he'd been told to take his feet off the chair. From early on, he disliked being constrained by other people's rules, and had an inbuilt urge to do things differently.

In the Fairfax band, Dizzy Gillespie met a superb trumpeter of his own age called Charlie Shavers. Shavers was obsessed with the trumpet playing of virtuoso Roy Eldridge, and he and Gillespie took every chance they could to listen to Eldridge on the radio, often in broadcasts from distant ballrooms like New York's Savoy. Eldridge, a diminutive but fiery trumpeter was six years older than Gillespie, and famous for his heated tone, clarity and speed across three octaves. He was the young brass players' model for the transitional period between swing and bop. Eldridge was inspired, like most of the era's jazz musicians, by Louis Armstrong, but he had matured in an era in which the fluent, effortless-seeming saxophone rather than the brasher trumpet, was prominent in jazz. Armstrong's improvisations were clear variations on the melody, while Eldridge departed further from the original tune, deploying a raspy growl (achieved by humming and playing at the same time). Eldridge was nickamed 'The Cat', and his work was a mix of showy exuberance and thrilling improvisation.

Although bebop was several years away, Eldridge already seemed to strive for something like it – a technically spectacular music in which the melodic swerves and turns were startling and abrupt. Eldridge didn't have a rich, lustrous, sound like Armstrong. His playing had an agitated quality, detectable in a constant reversion to the tremor and the shake, and to the use of high notes as introductions rather than climaxes. But Eldridge's underlying beat still sounded like swing.

Trumpeter Jon Faddis recalls:

'Dizzy took the language of Roy Eldridge and changed it all around. He changed the sense of phrasing, the sense of time, and the harmonic structure of song. So while his 1945 recording of "Blue 'n' Boogie" is still rhythmically influenced by Roy, it has this very different harmonic concept at work.'

In 1937 Gillespie left Philadelphia for New York. He went to all the jam sessions he could find, tried to get his face and his sound known, and eventually secured a job with bandleader Teddy Hill. He was hired for his musical resemblance to Eldridge, who had recently left the orchestra. Gillespie went on the road with Hill, touring France and Britain as well as the United States, and on his return he extended his interests to Afro-Cuban music,

Singer and bandleader Cab Calloway in 1943 with the Cotton Club Orchestra. Calloway knew that you didn't get big by hiding your light. He was one of the flashiest, and richest, showmen of the swing era, but he knew a good jazz musician when he heard one.

working with Cuban flautist Alberto Socarras. He also met Lorraine Willis, who later became his wife. Their relationship was to be the most stabilising influence in Gillespie's life until the end. They still spoke daily on the phone whenever the trumpeter was on tour.

Gillespie joined the Cab Calloway Orchestra in 1939, and by this time he was already a fine swing-band trumpeter, but he was beginning to answer the call of his own independent spirit. Joining Calloway turned out to be a stormy rite of passage, but from Calloway Gillespie learned that art and entertainment could be intimate friends.

Cabell 'Cab' Calloway was a remarkable phenomenon in a business already seething with quirky extroverts. He was the singing, dancing, wisecracking epitome of a jazz age in which the gap between spontaneous music and popular entertainment was much narrower than it is now. Calloway had unstoppable confidence, and his music always hovered on the brink of jazz. He also made sure that the musicians who worked for him were among the best in the business, and over the years many great jazz soloists emerged from the Calloway ranks, including Chu Berry, Ben Webster, and bassist Milt Hinton, as well as Gillespie.

'. . . from Calloway Gillespie learned that art and entertainment could be intimate friends.'

DIZZY GILLESPIE

The Calloway band in 1941. Dizzy Gillespie is the trumpeter standing on the left; he was already experimenting with bebop in late-night clubs after shows like this one finished.

Calloway is best known now for a selection of wacky novelty vocals, including his celebrated hit 'The Hi-De-Ho Man', which generated a hipster catchphrase that swept America during the 1930s. But although he was a showman, he liked jazz and jazz musicians. He was also an inspired vocalist, a skill easily eclipsed by his glitzy image. With his smooth articulation and immense range, Calloway represented something new on a jazz vocal scene hitherto dominated by the gravelly-voiced Armstrong. He made his name in the 1929 hit black musical *Hot Chocolates*, and in 1931 his band followed Duke Ellington's into the legendary Cotton Club.

Gillespie later recalled Calloway conducting his band, 'waving, shaking his head and making the hair fall down on his face'. Calloway also displayed an enthusiasm for Harlem's jive-talk culture that became a key aspect of the bebop lifestyle, and even published his own *Hepster's* (the original incarnation of 'hipster') *Dictionary*.

The Calloway experience was a rich one. Even if the young players took issue with the flashy Calloway manner, they couldn't fault the conditions it bought. Those good enough to get into the orchestra would find themselves moving from an average weekly wage of around $35 to $100, big money in 1936. In its heyday the band even travelled the States with its own private railroad car, a sought-after arrangement for the most successful black bands, because it meant a decent meal and a bed were possible even in the Southlands.

During his time with Calloway, Gillespie's interest in Cuban music was kindled through fellow-trumpeter Mario Bauza. He had also begun exploring more personal variations on the swing style in offstage improvisations with the band's virtuoso bassist Milt Hinton. Gillespie later said in an interview with the *Village Voice* that he believed Eldridge's style came 'from the trumpet itself', but in his own case it was his earliest love, the piano, that became central to his search for new methods. A sophisticated harmonic thinker from early on, Gillespie's relationship with the keyboard and the drum was crucial to his originality and to his capacity to share innovation with others. Gillespie believed he conceived melody in a drummer-like way, and became an excellent occasional conga player at his own gigs.

While on tour with Calloway in Kansas in 1940, Gillespie found the flame that lit his smouldering ambitions. He contacted his friend Buddy Anderson, a trumpeter with the local Jay McShann band. Anderson was anxious his friend should hear a new saxophone voice in town. 'Not another saxophone player!' Gillespie protested. But Anderson dragged Gillespie to hear a young alto saxophonist called Charlie Parker and – like countless musicians after him – Gillespie realised that this quiet, shambolic-looking young man was opening the next chapter in the story of jazz. Parker and Gillespie jammed all day at the Booker T. Washington Hotel in Kansas City. It was the beginning of the relationship that helped set the bebop revolution in motion.

BOP
FASHIONS

Bebop was a subculture as well as a musical revolution – it had its own language, its own ethics, its own mode of dress. But this early version of the Cult of Cool hadn't simply begun with Charlie Parker, Dizzy Gillespie and Thelonious Monk. Lester Young, the swing-era saxophone star of the Basie band, from whom Charlie Parker had drawn so much inspiration, was an inspirational hipster too, with his pork-pie hats, fondness for marijuana and eloquently minimalist private vocabulary.

But Gillespie, Parker, Monk and their contemporaries had grown up in a different era of black American culture. The Depression had stimulated a great deal of socialist analysis of American society, notably the way its inequalities rebounded particularly on blacks. Showbusiness habits that had grown up in the world of minstrels and vaudeville, a world of apparently carefree, obligingly exotic black entertainers in flashy clothes, didn't tally with a growing determination among black artists that something had to change. The beboppers took to more sober, conservative suits and ties, like Wall Street executives, but they added another layer from the intellectual milieu of modern art. They sported black berets and goatee beards like Parisian left-bank painters and horn-rimmed glasses like scholars and academics. But, as if to reflect the cutting-edge vitality and unpredictability of the evolving new jazz, they would add further touches such as a fez, a spotted bow tie, or shades. Sunglasses in particular helped to preserve an aura of emotional untouchability, as well as offering a surreal slant on the twilit world of the jazz club.

Wall Street meets the Left Bank on 52nd Street, New York. Dizzy Gillespie (right) was one of the leading role models in hipster and bebop fashions of the 1940s.

CHARLIE
PARKER

MILES DAVIS ONCE SAID that the history of jazz could be told in four words: 'Louis Armstrong, Charlie Parker'. Parker was an unruly, intuitive genius. At his peak, fresh musical ideas seemed to spring unquenchably from him, although he rarely bothered to write them down. This was the volatile fuel that propelled bebop and changed the way players all over the world conceived jazz. The late Ronnie Scott, tenor saxophonist and club proprietor, recalled that when he first heard a Charlie Parker record in the 1940s, it suddenly seemed 'the obvious way to play'.

Parker didn't scrap the rules on saxophone improvisation, but built new principles on the foundations of the old. Lester Young was his model, although he delivered Young's ideas at such a pace they were almost unrecognisable. Parker hurtled over the usual starting points and pauses of popular song-forms to produce uneven phrases of quirky lengths and odd resolutions in place of the flowing soliloquies of the swing musicians. He contrasted sustained sounds and bluesy wails with short sixteenth-notes, and would shift in mid-solo to unlikely keys from which it would seem he could never safely return, yet arrive back at his departure point without a blink.

Charles Christopher Parker was born in Kansas City on 29 August, 1920, and died in New York on 12 March, 1955. He was the son of a Kansas song-and-dance man and a doting mother, Addie Parker, who was responsible for the boy's upbringing, and who gave him his first saxophone. Charlie Parker's musical education and self-instruction was haphazard. He learned to play the instrument in all the keys, not knowing he wasn't expected to. However, although the local saxophone hero Lester Young was his biggest inspiration, he rapidly evolved his own style.

After work with local Kansas bands, Parker joined the successful Jay McShann Orchestra. His methods already reflected the harmonic departures, expansion and substitution of basic pop-song chords, and more unpredictable conception of rhythm that became his signature. Like Dizzy Gillespie, who he met in 1940, Parker began to share his insights with others at New York's Minton's Playhouse. He fitfully took up jobs with the Earl Hines, and then Billy Eckstine, bands but his addiction to narcotics and alcohol made some of these engagements brief. In 1945, he formed the prototype bebop band with alternations of Gillespie and Miles Davis (trumpets) and the virtuoso Max Roach on drums. Bebop classics emerged from these performances, such as the blues 'Now's the Time', 'Billie's Bounce' and 'Koko'. Many other classics, including 'Cheryl', 'Buzzy' and 'Parker's Mood', were recorded by the Savoy label over the next three years, as well as the brilliant 'Ornithology', 'Yardbird Suite', 'Night in Tunisia' and 'Cool Blues' for the west-coast Dial label between 1946 and 1948. Parker's work was documented between 1947 and 1948 by a follower of Parker's, Dean Benedetti, who recorded him on a portable acetate-cutting machine.

Parker's taut and lyrical music was a hit with the bop insiders but not with the wider public, and a series of romantic recordings with string accompaniment broadened his appeal in the early 1950s. But his inner life mingled visions of exquisite music with perceptions of turmoil, and he never managed to control his drug habit. Parker's remaining years were spent on musical one-night stands and work with unsuitable partners, and although he briefly enjoyed prestigious exposure with the Woody Herman and Stan Kenton bands, they were not suitable creative settings for him. Parker died at the age of 34 in the home of jazz patroness Baroness Pannonica de Koenigswarter, in paroxysms of laughter while watching TV. The examining doctor estimated his age at somewhere between 50 and 60.

Right: Charlie Parker watches and waits on a recording session in the 1940s. Parker's behaviour could be self-absorbed and erratic, yet he appreciated the music of others, whatever form it took.

2

DIZZY GILLESPIE

According to jazz historian James Lincoln Collier, Gillespie had already made progress towards a new music that is sometimes credited above all else to Charlie Parker's intuitive genius:

'Gillespie got very interested in the business of moving a half step, which wasn't done in jazz, say from an F chord to an E chord, and you can hear that as early as 1939 . . . He went on from there to work out a whole theory which would justify the use of these notes, where he would play a major chord over a minor . . . Calloway said "I don't like this Chinese music that you're playing". But a lot of the young musicians were getting very curious about it . . .

'. . . Now, why did he like that particular kind of movement? Well now you begin talking about Dizzy's personality, he was a very tough-minded guy in many respects, nobody was going to push him around . . . He had that kind of mischievous personality, but at bottom was a very serious guy. He liked the sound of something that was really not quite acceptable, although it had been acceptable in classical music for a long, long time. Stravinsky's "Rite of Spring" was already 25 years old, but this was certainly new in jazz and it was attracting a lot of attention.'

When Parker came to New York in the autumn of 1941, he and Gillespie pursued their musical experimentation in after-hours jam sessions, the focus of which eventually became Minton's Playhouse. Owner Henry Minton put Teddy Hill in charge of the musical policy and the playhouse became a retreat for bored young swing-band musicians. Hill hired drummer Kenny Clarke to liven the place up, and Clarke brought in a former gospel-pianist with a spiky, angular touch, Thelonious Sphere Monk.

'. . .New York was humming with players his own age who were developing their own angles on a new kind of jazz.'

Charlie Parker (left) with Gillespie at Birdland. The club was named in honour of Parker, whose nickname was 'Yardbird' or 'Bird'.

At Minton's, Gillespie discovered that New York was humming with players of his own age who were developing their own angles on a new kind of jazz. As well as Monk and Clarke, there was a harmonically sophisticated guitarist, Charlie Christian, who was one of 'King of Swing' Benny Goodman's star soloists. And now there was Charlie Parker, a saxophonist who seemed to resemble the swing hero Lester Young, but who played twice as fast. He was negotiating harmonic subtleties the other Minton's regulars had never encountered before.

Between them, these young players transformed jazz with music that not only based improvisation on multi-voiced augmented chords, but which changed the rhythmic emphasis so weak or unstressed accents in swing were dominant in bop. The feel of the beat shifted from the steady chug of the swing pulse to a more unpredictable, agitated style. The harmonies sounded strange and at times even discordant, tunes resembled standard songs turned inside out, or ended abruptly as if a door had been slammed on the proceedings.

In 1941, Gillespie lost his job with Cab Calloway's flamboyant outfit. If Calloway's *Hepster's Dictionary* and cultivated eccentricities made him hip in the minds of the general public, he wasn't hip enough for his young musicians, who would covertly send him up onstage. Gillespie was often the instigator of stunts like 'spitballing', hurling paper balls during the performance, but the trigger for the famous fight when Gillespie came at Calloway with a knife was, for once, not his fault. Calloway forgave him years later, when he found out his excitable trumpeter hadn't been the spitballer on this particular occasion, but it was the end of Gillespie's occupancy of Calloway's trumpet chair.

Gillespie then worked for several leaders, including Coleman Hawkins, Benny Carter and Earl Hines, but increasingly his most intense musical experiences were at Minton's. There between 1942 and 1944, in small-hours jam sessions and during rehearsals for mainstream swing bands, the bop vocabulary was honed and refined. Gillespie knew how to tell people exactly what he wanted, and wasn't apologetic about it, and this trait contributed immensely to his role as a guru of the evolving new art. Gillespie attributed the ambitious stylistic breakthroughs of bebop, what he simply called 'getting from one note to another', or 'the style of the thing', principally to Charlie Parker. He saw his own insights as being particularly associated with rhythm, evolutions of the experiments that he had already attempted with the bassist Milt Hinton and others.

Substituting complex chords, and more of them, for the chord changes of old songs was a favourite bop method. Gillespie heard an old standard called 'Whispering' when he was a teenager, and its chords became the basis of his classic early-bop composition 'Groovin' High' – but with four chords inserted for every one that had sufficed before. Gillespie's 1942 'Little John Special' solo is an unmistakable bebop break inserted into a conventional swing-band format, and the ensemble playing also includes a repeated riff that the trumpeter was to turn into the classic 'Salt Peanuts'.

'Little John Special' made it on to record, but most of the innovation of the next two years was undocumented, because during that period the American Federation of Musicians had imposed a recording strike in pursuit of better conditions. But the word was leaking out anyway.

MILES
DAVIS

Miles Davis, the trumpeter whose quiet, oblique style for much of his early career was the diametric opposite of Gillespie's — but who nevertheless influenced jazz as profoundly, and is still revered today.

ILES DAVIS'S TRUMPET SOUND was one of the few characteristic jazz sounds that could be recognised by listeners with little knowledge of the music or its practitioners. Frequently playing softly, close to the middle register, and often with his sound closeted by the mute, he veered between shy elusiveness and poised eloquence. The musical principles of tension and release, resolution and suspension, were more imaginatively realised by Miles Davis than by almost anyone else in the history of jazz. He changed his views about the best way to interpret these delicate principles several times, and thus acquired the reputation as an expander of jazz language, and a shrewd enabler of its performers' talents, as well as a gifted trumpet stylist.

Miles Dewey Davis was born in Alton, Illinois on 25 May 1926, and died of pneumonia and a stroke in California on 28 September 1991. Although his work went through many changes, his fundamental attitudes to jazz, ensembles and improvisation were coalescing by the end of the 1940s. A former Juilliard music-school student, Davis battled his way into Charlie Parker's quintet by a mixture of talent and persistence, replacing the departed Dizzy Gillespie, on whom he had based as much of his trumpet technique as he could. Davis wasn't as fast or as saxophone-like as Gillespie, and his early mature style mingled an elegant and more oblique version of bop's breathless runs with a softer sound and more spacy construction that highlighted variation of timbre.

In 1949, at the age of 23, Davis became nominal leader of a band devised by Gerry Mulligan and Gil Evans. The Birth of the Cool nonet reflected the tonal characteristics of his own style, mingled with late-romantic classical devices. The approach wasn't a commercial success, and in the early 1950s Davis's career took a steep downturn while he fought a battle against his addiction to hard drugs that he eventually won. At the 1955 Newport Jazz Festival, Davis made a spectacular comeback, and he was soon leading a band with a hurricane of a young saxophonist, John Coltrane.

Always uneasy with bebop's iconoclastic speediness, Davis now adopted the experiments of jazz composer and theoretician George Russell, exploring the use of cycles of scales ('modes') to improvise on, rather than the chord patterns of songs. The method imparted a more ambiguous, mysterious air to jazz pieces, reminiscent of Indian modal music. Davis had one of his biggest record successes in this guise, the famous 'Kind of Blue' session of 1960. Collaborations with Canadian 'Birth of the Cool' arranger Gil Evans also set Davis's moody, atmospheric trumpet voice against lustrous orchestral scores that avoided the slamming, exclamatory riffs of the pre-war big bands.

Always aware of his surroundings, Miles Davis negotiated a 1960s jazz environment that was increasingly polarised between largely structureless free-improvisation (the direction John Coltrane was drawn towards) and the popular appeal of funk and rock. He ran a superb quintet during this period, hiring a 16-year-old drummer (Tony Williams), plus the gifted Herbie Hancock on piano. This young man was comfortable with funk or classical concertos side by side, and had already had a hit with the Latin-jazz composition 'Watermelon Man'. The group was a model of loose collective spontaneity and offbeat themes, but Davis gradually moved closer to the world of pop and street funk, attracted to the sound of successful chart bands like Sly and the Family Stone. Electric funk albums under Davis's direction, like 'In A Silent Way' and 'Bitches Brew' followed, jazz instruments weaving in and out of restless electronic and percussion backdrops.

Disruptions in Davis's personal life diverted him through the late 1970s and into the 1980s: car crashes, mental and physical crises, a long layoff from playing and manic pursuits of sex and cocaine. He made a number of attractive, if less improvisationally challenging, records during the 1980s, sometimes in the company of imaginative new pop-jazz conceptualists like bassist-composer Marcus Miller. His death in 1991 left a massive gap in the world of late-20th-century music. His one-time bassist, British virtuoso Dave Holland, reflected at the time: 'Miles was a direct link to Bird (Charlie Parker), and that means so much to young players in itself. But he was also open to the sounds they've heard, Motown and James Brown as well as Bird. And he was a master of creating the conditions for something to happen.'

Dizzy Gillespie loved Cuban music and insisted that the source of both it and jazz was always 'Mother Africa'. His 1948 big band powerfully featured 'cubop', notably through the brilliant percussionist Chano Pozo (centre). Saxophonist and long-time friend James Moody is on the left.

Bassist Oscar Pettiford joined Gillespie to form the first indisputably bop-oriented band to play on New York's jazz boulevard, 52nd Street. From 1944 through the following year a growing coterie of mostly young jazz fans began to treat the newcomers, particularly Charlie Parker, as the messengers of a new age from a far galaxy.

Earl Hines' singer Billy Eckstine, a glamorous and velvet-voiced performer who became the first black pop star of national status, formed his own bop orchestra, and hired Gillespie as his musical director. The first bop recordings involving like-minded small groups were made around the same time, some with members of Coleman Hawkins' band, some with a group that was fronted by Gillespie and Charlie Parker. Bop anthems like 'Salt Peanuts' and 'Hot House' were recorded – but on small independent labels that had come to life during

the recording ban, not on the suspicious or indifferent majors. Bop's detractors thought it was a deliberately obscure, discordant and unswinging music that would be briefly fashionable with a handful of wackos and bohemians. For the more enlightened it was a magical transformation of familiar jazz materials into something purer, quicker, hotter, more incisive and demanding, and indifferent to the blandishments of showbusiness.

Jon Faddis recalls Gillespie's perceptions of those years:

'Dizzy said that Charlie Parker told him Dizzy's heart beat on one beat, and Charlie Parker's heart beat on the next beat, that's how close they were . . . the way they played together sounded like one person. The phrasing was very, very precise.

'Charlie Parker showed Dizzy a way of playing that almost eliminated that swing feel that Dizzy had in the early '40s, but that also incorporated those harmonic ideas that they both created. So I think the way of getting from one note to the next was very much Charlie Parker's influence on Dizzy. But if Charlie Parker was the stylist, Dizzy was sort of the architect that taught the musicians how to build the music . . . Dizzy said that Charlie Parker used to come over to his house, and Dizzy's wife Lorraine wouldn't let him in, so Charlie Parker would be in the hallway playing and Dizzy would write it down, and then show it to the other musicians. So Dizzy took the things that Charlie Parker thought of off the top of his head – Dizzy said he never saw him sit at the piano – and he would show other musicians.'

Gillespie's relationship with Charlie Parker eventually foundered as a result of the latter's chaotic personal life, unreliability and drug abuse. Parker's appetites for most known forms of physical gratification became almost as legendary as his capacity for spontaneous saxophone invention, but Gillespie – for all his reputation for mischief – was shrewd in business, meticulous in time-keeping, and disciplined about booze and drugs.

James Lincoln Collier affirms:

'Dizzy Gillespie and Charlie Parker were two entirely different kinds of people, Charlie Parker was a guy who obviously had emotional problems, he was ruthless with his friends, he was always borrowing people's horns and then hocking them, going off with their suits, whatever he needed he took, he was a terrible drug user, he drank a great deal, he had severe emotional difficulties. Dizzy Gillespie was . . . an intelligent, mature guy who knew how to handle his career, he knew how to manipulate showbusiness people around him, and that's pretty tough because those showbusiness people are in the business of manipulating artists. He came out of it not necessarily rich but certainly very, very comfortable and one of the most famous jazz musicians in the world.'

Finally leaving Parker and his chaotic lifestyle behind, Dizzy Gillespie applied both his musical and his business acumen to the notion of organising his first big band in 1945, to accompany a famous dance duo, the Nicholas Brothers. Gillespie liked the big band sound, but he also knew it was popular with a less specialised audience than small-group bop, and he thought the change might broaden bop's appeal and his own economic base into the bargain. But the first time around, it was a financial disaster. A year later, he tried again with better luck. He recorded expanded bebop arrangements like 'Things To Come' and 'Emanon', found enthusiastic followers in Europe, and rekindled his enthusiasm for Latin American rhythms. The Cubop classic 'Manteca' emerged from a collaboration between Gillespie and his conga player Chano Pozo. 'Cubana Be, Cubana Bop' emerged from an Africanised opening rhythmic fragment from Pozo, expanded by Gillespie and finally resolved by former drummer George Russell's fully worked composition.

Gillespie was forced to wind the big band up in 1950 – postwar belt-tightening forced many famous orchestras into insolvency or at least into contraction, even Count Basie's. However, its legacy has spectacularly stood the test of time, and the pieces are still played frequently.

Gillespie reverted to playing with small groups during this period. He was briefly employed as a star soloist with the eclectic Stan Kenton Orchestra, and equally briefly ran his own independent record label, Dee Gee. He worked frequently with one of the few large-scale jazz ventures still keeping its head above water – impresario Norman Granz's Jazz At The Philharmonic touring package. Whether or not the jazz world was in a more fragile condition than it had been, Dizzy Gillespie had become a legend. For the most casual consumer of musical news he would have been a phenomenon for those ballooning cheeks and his bellows-like neck alone, but in 1953 he added to his stock of memorable mannerisms by adopting a unique new trumpet, on which the bell slanted diagonally upward at 45 degrees to its regular position. Jon Faddis said:

'I don't think there was anything that Dizzy could do to not puff his cheeks, and I don't think it was something that he did because he thought it looked hip, I just think that that's what he had to do in order to produce the music, and that's what worked for him, although it doesn't work for everyone. He said, "When I heard Charlie Parker, that's when I started doing it." Charlie Parker used to tell him to say, "Two thousand, two hundred and twenty two" because every time he would say those hard "T"s his neck would just – two thousand, two hundred and twenty two – would bulge out like that.'

And the 45-degree trumpet bell?

'Dizzy was at a party for his wife, Lorraine – I think it

was '53, or '54 – and he'd left his straight trumpet on a trumpet stand, and he went, in the middle of the party, to do an interview. One of a comedy team at the party pushed the other one, hit the trumpet and instead of the bell crushing and compacting, the trumpet ended up with the bell sticking up. Dizzy played it and he sort of liked what he heard, he felt there was a better way to hear himself as a trumpeter. He asked his instrument company at that time, the Martin Company, if they could make him one, and history was made.'

In 1956 he had another opportunity to lead a big band, and with it came the beginnings of the trumpeter's role as international jazz globetrotter. That year a Gillespie orchestra undertook two world tours for the US State Department, visiting Pakistan, Lebanon, Syria, Iran, Turkey, Yugoslavia, Greece and Latin America. The tours were a considerable success and enabled Gillespie to keep a big band viable for another two years. This was a time of expansion of America's cultural boundaries, and Gillespie's international role as a jazz ambassador made him popular with a succession of US Presidents, and he performed several times at the White House. He did, however, maintain with some vigour that he should be President himself, and Miles Davis head of the CIA.

During the early 1960s, Gillespie's pianist was the Argentinian composer Lalo Schifrin, who was subsequently to write a number of sympathetic pieces showcasing the leader's increasingly mellow and evocative trumpet sound. In the mid 1960s, Gillespie's work with small groups acquired an empathy and elegant swing that was imposing even by his own high standards. The saxophonist James Moody, an unquenchably inventive old associate from the 1940s big band, who also shared Gillespie's appetite for surrealism, was a constantly exhilarating presence. Gillespie also embarked on more idiosyncratic and personal projects,

like improvising a solo trumpet backdrop for a movie about the Dutch painter Karel Appel, which won first prize at the Berlin Film Festival.

Jazz music in general suffered a downturn with the progressive rock boom of the later 1960s and the repercussions of this reached Dizzy Gillespie just like everyone else. He recorded less, but worked again with Gil Fuller, his arranger from the 1940s big band. He also participated in music education projects on television, and by the early 1970s he was working with the Giants of Jazz, an all-star touring group including Thelonious Monk.

'. . . James Moody . . . also shared Gillespie's appetite for surrealism . . .'

By the mid-1970s, bebop was growing popular again, a belated embrace for what was finally being seen as a classic American art form whose originators deserved gratitude while many of them were still creatively active. In 1974, Gillespie re-established a close relationship with his old Jazz At The Philharmonic boss Norman Granz, this time signing with Granz's new company Pablo Records and resuming a busy recording schedule.

The following year, Dizzy Gillespie's musical achievements were celebrated at New York's Avery Fisher Hall in an evening of big-band and small group performances that reunited him with many old associates of the previous three decades. America's Institute of High Fidelity asked his one-time disciple Miles Davis to present him with its Musician of the Year Award.

The Pablo Records deal allowed much of Gillespie's later style to be recorded including *Jazz At The Philharmonic* showbiz encounters. Gillespie was put in a 'Trumpet Kings' setting with Roy Eldridge, Clark Terry, Harry Edison and others. Some recordings bring the newcomer Jon Faddis to the fore. These are fascinating examples of dedication to a hero's style, but are also interesting for the ways the young Faddis could assert his own personality.

Over the coming decade, with a global renaissance of interest in bebop, Gillespie took to the road and the schedule probably made regular recording harder, although a variety of live sessions still charted his progress. The 1980s culminated in a sensational duet between Dizzy Gillespie and the veteran bebop drum colossus Max Roach, at Montreux in 1989 – a session in which neither man paid even the most cursory attention to the passing of the years or the possible waning of their powers, and in which jazz music's spirit of spontaneity and surprise was jubilantly celebrated.

For his 75th birthday in October 1992, Dizzy Gillespie was booked for eight weeks into the Blue Note club in Greenwich Village, scheduled to perform with a wide variety of musicians who had been important in his life, or who he had influenced. Not long after this event, which meant a great deal to him, Dizzy Gillespie entered hospital and was diagnosed as suffering from cancer of the pancreas. He died the following January.

Jon Faddis observes:

'Dizzy used to like to think of himself as working in the service of humanity. And I think that was what he did. He'd taught Max Roach, he'd taught Miles Davis, he taught Fats Navarro, Benny Harris, Kenny Dorham, Red Rodney, me, Freddie Hubbard, Clifford Brown – he worked with all of us to show what he was doing, and what the music was. Our jobs were to take that, and then do it in our own way. Try to develop it, and then, when young musicians come up to us, to help them in the same way.'

Danilo Perez, the pianist who joined Gillespie's band in 1989 and worked with him to the end, confirms the

'You know what I'm sayin?' Dizzy at the Kool Jazz Festival in Saratoga in 1981. The bent trumpet came about by accident, but he preferred the sound it made.

impact the trumpeter had on all who worked with him and shared his love of music and life:

'He taught me so much about music and about life, that no matter what happens in the life, in the music you get better, and become better, and stay just the same person. You talk to everybody, you look at people for what they are. He was an unbelievable spirit and a genius.'

3

THELONIOUS MONK

'If there's one person of whom I can say, unequivically, that this man never compromised . . . never even thought of betraying his art, that man would be Thelonious Monk.'

ORRIN KEEPNEWS, RECORD PRODUCER

3 THELONIOUS MONK

Thelonious Sphere Monk in the 1940s. Even in jazz, an idiom full of single-minded individuals, Monk was utterly uncompromising from the beginning.

Today Thelonious Monk's music is revered, and his work is played by jazz performers of all ages and persuasions for its continuing freshness and distinctiveness. It is also played and recorded by contemporary classical ensembles as unique examples of 20th-century African-American music. Monk's single-mindedness made all that possible. Producer Orrin Keepnews, who oversaw Monk's remarkable later work on the Riverside label, says 'If there's one person of whom I can say, unequivocally, that this man never compromised, this man never even thought of betraying or watering down his art, that man would be Thelonious Monk.' In upmarket concert halls, jazz clubs, on supermarket muzak tapes, or the sound-systems of restaurants and winebars, the unexpected hairpin turns and the hopping, fragmentary progress of a Monk melody – and the craggily elegant designs of his pieces – is now firmly established in the late 20th-century soundscape.

Monk appeared to play the piano with all the bone and muscle in his body, splaying his elbows, prodding at the keyboard with his fingers flattened and his forearms jabbing, at times rising from the stool as if to put even more of his bearlike frame behind the impact. When he settled into the clanking, skittering runs that were his notion of straight-ahead swing, his feet flapped wildly like marionettes, apparently controlled by wires directed by some source other than the mysterious, unreachable mind under his remarkable assortment of hats.

Sometimes he would get up and commence a preoccupied lurch and stagger around the stage, weaving as if sparring with an invisible opponent – and always in synchronicity, or else in some oppositional tempo, with whatever else was going on in his band. Casual witnesses assumed this was simply one of Monk's many eccentricities, or a sign that he was absorbed by the work of his colleagues, since there were usually few facial

'Monk appeared to play the piano with all the bone and muscle in his body . . .'

Monk, for once with no hat, at the Downbeat Club on 52nd Street in 1944, along with two of the all-time great swing saxophonists, Coleman Hawkins (left) and Don Byas (centre). Hawkins and Byas were nevertheless broad-minded enough to appreciate bebop.

indications of his feelings. But more regular devotees suspected that it was Monk's way of conducting the band. A few believed the behaviour derived from his teenage experience of performing with evangelists, where uninhibited physical responses were almost obligatory.

Monk's music was sharply criticised by observers, the general public and many of his fellow musicians during the first decade of his emergence as a soloist and composer in the 1940s. Many of the criticisms were variations on the familiar theme of that period, that modern jazz didn't respect a melody, and didn't swing. However, of all the wilful leaders of the 1940s' bebop movement, Monk appeared the least affected by this torrent of negative attention. Most of the boppers avoided flash showbiz antics and on-stage pranks and made the mannerisms of serious artistry part of their act, as a way of establishing their independence from vaudeville and the dancehall world inhabited by their

3 THELONIOUS MONK

predecessors. Yet, compared to the hyper-cool Miles Davis, none was more obviously indifferent to the presence, absence, enthusiasm or indifference of an audience than Thelonious Monk. His work conveyed the unmistakable impression that the music he made didn't seem odd to him, and if it seemed odd to others he couldn't help that.

Orrin Keepnews endorses this assessment:

'I think that one of the most wonderful and exciting and remarkable things about Monk was his tremendous confidence in himself and his tremendous ability to go full speed ahead without regard for other consequences or without regard for whether what he was doing was being appreciated. Now, there's an important point to be recognised about Monk in relationship to his own genius – I seriously believe that Monk did not understand that his music was difficult. He understood it, he had a perfect grasp of what it was about, how come you didn't?'

Thelonious Monk's most striking and lasting compositions were written in the first stages of his career, during the emergent bebop movement of the 1940s, during his period of eclipse and resurgence as a leader. 'Round Midnight' was to become not only one of the best-known of all jazz tunes, but also the title that seemed to resonate with that atmosphere of smoky basements, after-hours exotica and lowlife creativity so beloved of jazz mythology; and, in the late 1980s, it became the title of a jazz feature film by the French director Bertrand Tavernier. It was recorded and interpreted by jazz musicians as different as Miles Davis, saxophonists Sonny Rollins and Steve Lacy, fusion guitarist Stanley Jordan, British classical pianist Joanna McGregor, and even the bandleader Sun Ra – an artist who could legitimately claim to be even more formidably indifferent to mainstream taste than Monk himself.

Monk was a genius at the subversion of expectations, and at delaying or diverting resolutions that appeared to be imminent and inevitable. He also introduced such

'Monk did not understand that his music was difficult. He understood it . . . how come you didn't?'

ORRIN KEEPNEWS

harmonic richness and ambiguity into his compositions that they offered immense potential for remoulding, for being harmonised and reharmonised in as many ways as new interpreters might choose to explore it. Improvising players could challenge the limits of their own skills and sensibilities, yet however much they might make the tune sound like them, it would also always sound like Monk too, and, moreover, sound like jazz. More than almost any other jazz composer, Monk drew his inspiration from African-American traditions alone – from blues, church music, swing, boogie, and bebop.

If 'Round Midnight' was Thelonious Monk's most popular composition, such other early masterpieces as 'Evidence', 'Criss Cross' and 'Misterioso' are not far behind. Their urgent, spiky melodies, interrogatory exchanges between fundamental motifs and subtle alteration of the same phrase by repeating it in different rhythmic patterns still retain their vigour. Yet Monk could also apply his wayward principles to more standard material; his account of 'Smoke Gets In Your Eyes' certainly does not bury the familiar melody, but takes on a spare and guttural quality that is quite different from the original.

With later compositions like 'Crepuscule with Nellie' (dedicated to his wife) and 'Gallop's Gallop', Thelonious Monk confirmed how exhilaratingly he could stretch the envelope of what traditionally counted as 'right' or 'wrong' notes, and with the 1956 recording Brilliant

GOSPEL
CHURCHES

AMERICA'S BAPTIST AND METHODIST Churches were the first in the country to reconsider the prevailing 18th-century argument that the slave population was too primitive to be admitted into Christianity in the New World. However, in embracing the slaves and welcoming them into their community, the churches found themselves absorbing much of the African ritual they were setting out to replace.

West African religious rituals involving movement and dance, spirit possession and 'getting religion' brought a kind of church life into being that has influenced the world's music throughout this century, and still does today. Jazz, soul music, blues and rock 'n' roll are all close relatives of it. Thelonious Monk's famous onstage shuffle-dance bears an uncanny resemblance to the collective movements of 19th-century 'ring-shouts', where worshippers would rhythmically shuffle around in a ring, therefore evading Christian disapproval of dancing in church by taking its definition of 'crossed feet' literally. Syncopated handclapping got around the problem of a widespread church ban on drums. The 'call-and-response' interchanges of gospel music and jazz evolved from the congregation's rhythmic echo of the preacher's words, and the slurred intonations and skewed-pitch techniques that so changed conventional hymn-singing were directly traceable to West Africa.

L.D. Frazier, a singer-pianist and travelling evangelist of the 1990s, understands how that environment in the 1930s might have affected the teenage Thelonious Monk and the distinctive development of his music:

'In West Africa, the Griot is the storyteller. The storyteller would be telling stories to the tribe, and as he would tell the story they would make comments. In today's gospel church, if a Baptist or Pentecostal minister says "Yes, and Jesus was talking to the multitude", the crowd reply "Oh yeah, we know what you are talking about". . .'

Frazier relates that phenomenon to Monk's characteristic use of oppositional or conversational phrasing in his music. He placed statement against a counter-statement or a complementary statement, a fragment of music echoed by a following fragment subtly altered as if by another voice. Frazier also makes the connection between church life and the individuality and forthrightness of a jazz solo: 'I've cried sometimes, uncontrollably, and I apologise to the audience. And they say, "Don't apologise just go on and be yourself".'

The interaction between preacher and audience, as in this Baptist service, appears in the conversational qualities of much jazz, gospel and blues. Black church music was crucial to Monk's development as it was to many jazz musicians.

THE
STRIDE PIANO

THE STRIDE PIANO STYLE rose to popularity in New York in the second decade of the 20th century. Stride was drawn from ragtime but greatly extended its scope and its potential as a vehicle for spontaneous playing. Ragtime, although a composed and not improvisational form of music, and heavily dependent on European classical forms, was out of step with its European parents in one crucial way: it reversed the usual stresses in the rhythm, and its name was derived from the description of its syncopated beat – 'ragged time'.

The Harlem 'stride school' was the most famous exponent of stride piano and included spectacular piano stars like Luckyeth Roberts, Willie 'The Lion' Smith, and James P. Johnson. These keyboard virtuosi prided themselves on invincible techniques, were heroes in their community, and often played at Harlem 'rent parties' where the local residents would charge entrance fees to their apartments to raise cash for the rent.

Stride was usually fast, and often reflected the players' schooled classical erudition in its right-hand melodic figures, while the left hand maintained an insistent, pumping rhythmic figure, alternating a reverberating bass note with a mid-register chord. James P. Johnson's 1921 'Carolina Shout' was one of the most famous of all stride piano solos, but Johnson's fame was quickly eclipsed by that of his even more remarkable pupil, Thomas 'Fats' Waller, a phenomenal technician who also became a much-loved 1930s pop star.

The most celebrated and spectacular descendent of the Harlem school was Art Tatum. The Ohio-born piano sensation was as much admired by classical virtuosi as by jazz players, and he was probably the fastest and most elaborate jazz pianist of all time. Inspired by the music of Fats Waller, Tatum produced a cascade of improvisation in which the harmonic underpinnings of the song were as likely to be spontaneously transformed as the melody itself – yet the rhythmic drive of stride was often fiercely sustained. The Harlem 'striders' influenced many pianists of all styles, including Thelonious Monk, and were also the inspiration for celebrated pianist-leaders such as Count Basie and Duke Ellington.

The great James P. Johnson, one of the kings of stride piano. Johnson's driving rhythms and powerful left hand came straight from the roots of ragtime and jazz, yet his melodic variations reflected his classical training.

Corners, he embarked on his most audacious manipulations of conventional scales, intervals, rhythm and space.

Although the arrangements were at times too taxing even for colleagues of the calibre of Monk's childhood friend Sonny Rollins on tenor saxophone and Clark Terry on trumpet (there were 25 attempts at the title track, and even then the album version had to be stitched together from different takes), the disc was very popular by the jazz-sales standards of the mid-1950s, and it helped to re-establish Monk's reputation after a period of isolation and neglect.

Thelonious Monk's impact on the music of our time and times to come may stem from his originality as a composer, but a characteristic of many of his pieces, whatever instruments they are played on, is that their sound powerfully echoes the sound of the piano. Monk's piano style derives from the Harlem 'stride school' of the 1920s, a technique derived from ragtime in which the right hand improvises freely on materials from styles as disparate as blues and the European classics, while the left 'strides' rhythmically between an alternated bass note and chord. His use of repeated phrases, varying slightly in intonation and rhythm from one instance to the next, reflects his experience in the chanting, incantatory musical environments of the Baptist Church.

Monk's touch at the keyboard was also different from that of most conventionally trained pianists. Classical pianists who subsequently adopted his music admit that they have to adapt it to their own techniques, rather than try to emulate the broken rules and rejections of piano orthodoxy that litter his playing. Monk played with his fingers flattened, and the backs of his hands curved in the reverse direction to the recommendations of any piano textbook; he also played very percussively, and liked hitting adjoining notes simultaneously with a drum-like impact, creating a dissonant effect that still made structural sense in his pieces. This was all a part of Monk's concept of melody, motion, harmony and rhythm. Danilo Perez, the ex-Dizzy Gillespie pianist whose work has been influenced by Monk's piano style and Latin-American rhythmic notions, says:

'That intensity of rhythms with blues, that kind of drum playing, he did that like nobody else did. He brought the rhythms, the sound of the piano too, but also the percussive side, you know, the piano as drums.'

Thelonious Sphere Monk's early life is a thinly documented subject, largely because the primary witness was rarely interviewed and disliked discussing his life and work. He was born in Rocky Mount, North Carolina, on 11 October 1917, but his family brought him to New York when he was four and he grew up in the San Juan Hill area of the city. His mother sang in the choir at the

> **'That intensity of rhythms with blues, that kind of drum playing, he did that like nobody else did.'**
>
> DANILO PEREZ

local Baptist Church, but if she had a more prominent part, her son would accompany her on piano. When the young Thelonious began to branch out in the music world, starting to frequent the low-life haunts where jazz was often played, his mother frequently went with him.

'My mother never figured I should do anything else', Monk told the British critic and photographer Valerie Wilmer in the 1960s. 'She was with me. If I wanted to play music, it was all right with her.' When he left home at 17 to tour with an evangelist preacher and play the Baptist churches for two years it's likely that the devout Mrs Monk approved, and the pianist described the experience to Valerie Wilmer as 'a lot of fun. When I got through, I'd had enough of church, though. I was in there practically every night. But I always did play jazz. In the churches I was playing music the same way. But I wouldn't say I'm religious.'

The great pianist and composer Mary Lou Williams recalled the teenage Thelonious Monk in the mid-1930s, encountering him in Kansas City on the evangelist's tour, and remarking in the British jazz and pop weekly *Melody Maker* in 1954:

> "When Monk was in Kaycee he jammed every night; really used to blow on piano, employing a lot more technique than he does today. Monk plays the way he does now because he got fed up . . . he felt that musicians should play something new, and started doing it. Most of us admire him for this. He was one of the original modernists all right. Only in those days we called it "Zombie music", and reserved it mostly for musicians after-hours.'

The bebop style was forged in those after-hours sessions, as younger musicians bored by the regimentation and show-business antics of the swing bands sought a purer and more technically challenging music that still powerfully reflected jazz's roots in syncopation and the blues. And of all the after-hours joints in the States where such experiments could occur at the dawn of the 1940s, the most famous was to be Minton's Playhouse, in New York's Harlem.

Thelonious Monk was first recorded there in 1941. Live recordings in those days were limited in quality, and Monk's piano is almost inaudible. However what can be heard reveals the distinct influence of the swing piano masters. Monk's primary source appeared to be Art Tatum, the dazzling piano virtuoso of the 1930s who made the instrument virtually a stand-alone jazz band. The link was in the connection of these early jazz keyboard stylists to the 'orchestral' methods of the New Orleans 'piano professors' of the turn of the century, and the Harlem stride-school virtuosi who followed them – resourceful performers adapting classically schooled techniques to vernacular uses. Monk may have grown increasingly spare and minimalist as his music evolved, but the interweaving of harmonic layers and counter-melodies came from the influence of pianists who played 'all' the instrument – an enthusiasm he shared with another jazz genius, Duke Ellington.

Monk also liked Earl 'Fatha' Hines, an ebullient stride-derived pianist from Pittsburgh of whirlwind speed and a dazzling independence who, during his close but competitive relationship with Armstrong in the 1920s,

'I wasn't thinking about trying to change the course of jazz, I was just trying to play something that sounded good' THELONIOUS MONK

invented what came to be called the 'trumpet style': linear, horn-like right hand lines and a trumpet-like trill.

But Monk's waywardness of spirit was leading him to reject a possibly lucrative career as a Tatum or Hines clone. The same conviction that drew Charlie Parker, Dizzy Gillespie and other young musicians to the New York jamming joints – the conviction that it was time for jazz to change fundamentally – gripped Monk before he even arrived in the city.

PIANO GIANTS OF
THE 1940S

Earl Hines

Earl 'Fatha' Hines was born in Pennsylvania in 1903, grew up in Pittsburgh, and was leading his own band in Chicago at the age of 21. He was almost as big a jazz celebrity as Louis Armstrong (with whom he had an active, and often productive rivalry) in the 1920s, and developed a soloistic piano technique of strong single-line melodies and vibrato-like trills in the right hand that came to be known as the 'trumpet' style. Hines constantly stretched and suspended the chugging regularity of 1920s jazz rhythms, quickly embraced the more fluid 1930s style of swing and, unlike Armstrong, was not dismissive of bebop. One of the undisputed jazz piano geniuses, Hines stayed on the road for most of his life, and had played at the White House and for the Pope by the time he died at the age of 79.

Mary Lou Williams

Another Pittsburgh piano star, influenced by Earl Hines, and a gifted composer and arranger as well as a keyboard virtuoso, Mary Lou Williams worked with the Andy Kirk swing-band during the 1930s, and gave it a prominence it would never have had without her – she also wrote scores for the most celebrated bandleaders of the day, including Earl Hines, Benny Goodman and later Duke Ellington and Dizzy Gillespie. A sophisticated harmonic thinker, Williams understood bebop and was friendly with many of its leading practitioners, including Thelonious Monk whom she had met in Kansas City. Stride playing and boogie woogie were important elements in her style, but overlaid by a graceful, mobile melodic flow – and driven by a boldness of outlook that even led to duets with gurus of the 1960s avant-garde such as Cecil Taylor. A devout Christian, Williams also wrote several sacred works.

Teddy Wilson

Born in Austin, Texas, Teddy Wilson was one of the most elegant and restrained of all swing-era pianists, anticipating the understatement of the postwar Cool School. The Chicago clubs of the late 1920s were Wilson's academy, and although his parents were middle-class, he was determined to become a full-time jazz musician. Wilson and piano legend Art Tatum began working together, and Tatum's fame was good exposure for the newcomer. Impresario John Hammond noticed Wilson, which led to him finding work with bandleader Benny Carter, highly successful recordings for the new jukebox market with Billie Holiday, and eventually the Benny Goodman Orchestra – Wilson was one of the first black jazz artists to work with a white band. Influenced by Hines, Wilson nevertheless had a distinctive harmonic language of his own, often concealing the harmonic basis of a chord in a way that prefigured bop.

Bud Powell

A Monk protége, Bud Powell quickly became a cornerstone of many pioneering bebop bands. Although the virtuosity of both Art Tatum and Teddy Wilson was no problem to him, Powell used his prodigious skill in a different way – playing very fast sax-like lines in the right hand, nudged and corralled by spare chord support, or 'comping', in the left hand. Powell altered the harmonic architecture of his left-hand chords to use unfamiliar and often dissonant intervals (a method that he shared with Thelonious Monk, but not foregrounded as part of the composition as Monk would do), and his phrasing was consistently surprising, and variable in texture from minimalist to Tatumesque onslaughts. But Bud Powell's career was hampered for many years by mental illness (possibly attributed to head injuries sustained as the result of a racial attack) and alcoholism, and he died in New York at the age of 41. The jazz movie *Round Midnight* uses elements of Powell's life in its storyline.

3 THELONIOUS MONK

Monk informed Valerie Wilmer in the book *Jazz People*:

'The music at Minton's just happened, I was playing there, so the others just used to come down and play with me. I guess they dug what I was doing. It was always crowded there, people enjoying themselves all the time . . . I wasn't thinking about trying to change the course of jazz, I was just trying to play something that sounded good. I never used to talk about it with other people, but I believe the other musicians did. It just happened.'

But although Monk's radical approach to existing jazz materials drew him towards other musical radicals who were developing the bop language, he avoided a

Thelonious Monk took the brilliant young player Bud Powell (left) under his wing in the 1940s, but where Monk played less, Powell played more: he was a dazzling bebop virtuoso, although alcohol cut short his career.

Monk (right) resisted bop's temptations to technical bravura – he was the most direct and focused of musicians, using the instrument to convey what he wanted to say and no more.

widespread inclination within the movement to emulate the fast single-note patterns of a bop horn-player like Parker or Gillespie. Bud Powell, the other central figure in modern jazz piano, developed an approach in which fast, legato right-hand runs were supported by the minimalist 'comping' of a left hand providing sporadic chords and contrasting accents. Jason Rebello, a piano star of the contemporary British scene, marvels at Monk's single-mindedness in resisting the flow:

'Monk's a complete individual, he didn't care about what people thought about him, he did things in his own way, and he even said, "Do things in your way, and if it takes the public twenty years to catch up, then that's fine". He plays with a technique that would make all the piano teachers I've had say, "Oh no, you can't play like that" – you know, really flat fingers, he didn't play fast, he didn't play flashy, everything he did was most definitely not to impress, but maybe to shock. But he was a very direct player, completely to the point, he wasn't concerned with doing any sort of pianistic flourishes. In fact probably the best way to say is, that he wasn't a pianist; he was a musician. He just used the piano to convey musically what he wanted to say, and that was it.'

Monk stubbornly retained a stripped-down version of a pre-bop piano method. He phased out his Tatum-style fast playing just as hurtling virtuosity was becoming

3

Monk at the piano, with Charlie Parker on alto sax and Roy Haynes on drums, at Minton's famous Playhouse. But although Monk was a bop founder, he was too quirky to be a popular accompanist.

popular in the new jazz. His timing and placement were becoming so unpredictably personal that only those partners who were used to playing with him could keep track of where they were. In the hands of Charlie Parker and Dizzy Gillespie, bop was becoming such a melodically mercurial music that the rhythm section needed to retain a firmly implied, underlying beat to sustain the scheme. Thelonious Monk was far too wayward to be relied on for that. He also made the dissonances in his harmonies far more exposed and emphatic than those of his contemporaries and even to more adventurous ears the music sounded just too weird for comfort.

The jazz historian James Lincoln Collier observes:

'In many cases Monk's melody lines really are very, very simple, just as basic as they could be. A lot of what you have in Monk comes from displaced accents, metric shifts, . . . Monk's method was to play notes in unexpected places as opposed to the very busy, complex bebop style where Parker and Gillespie were playing a mile a minute, tempos up around three hundred which is faster than most people can play. Yet Monk was playing really this very, very simple stuff where the musical meaning depended upon this displacement of notes. Not that he didn't use dissonance, of course he did, a lot of seconds and minor seconds too, but it was that simplicity with that very angular feel to it that marked his music and that was very different from bebop.'

Danilo Perez, the young Panamanian pianist profoundly influenced by Monk's methods, endorses the notion that it wasn't what he was doing, but how he was doing it, that got the results. Perez explains:

'In just a very simple framework of four beats, one-two-three-four, he will take the same idea or phrase and repeat it, and each time he'll start in the second beat, then in the third beat, the same idea in the fourth beat, so he'll take the same little thing and keep moving it around. That's brilliant because he could make a solo of two or three choruses just with one idea or just one note.'

Monk's approach to the piano certainly made it apparent that he was a distinctive stylist early on, but he was becoming a stylist in a school that only he attended. Monk's endlessly patient mother helped support him through the economic pressures this stance occasioned, a nurturing relationship that was extended when he married his childhood friend and neighbour Nellie, who first worked at a variety of clerical jobs and then took in sewing when their first child was born, to keep Monk's muse from the distractions of the material world.

As with many things that didn't involve a keyboard or score-sheet, Monk appeared unaware of this. As he said to Valerie Wilmer: 'I didn't notice it too much. I had certain things to do. I wasn't starving or nothing.' Nellie Monk confirmed that single-mindedness: 'Music to him is work,' she said. 'When he wasn't working regularly, he'd be working at home, writing and rehearsing bands that didn't have the prospects of a dog. He just did it to know what it would sound like.'

But if Monk had no notion of how to sell his increasingly unusual wares, and almost certainly would

Thelonious Monk's headgear was almost as famous as the characteristic clang of his piano chords. He often performed as if in a world of his own.

not have bothered even if he had, he had supporters in high places, and not all of them in the bebop priesthood either. Coleman Hawkins, the pioneer of the tenor saxophone as a solo instrument rather than a vaudeville special-effects device, was a sophisticated harmonic improvisor, spinning spontaneous melody off a song's chords rather than embroidering its theme. Hawkins was sympathetic to bebop's development of this, and he heard harmonies in Monk's music that appealed to him.

Hawkins hired Monk in 1944, and recorded with him in a quartet.

'. . . he could make a solo of two or three choruses with just one idea, or just one note.' DANILO PEREZ

MONK'S
PARTNERS

MANY HORN PLAYERS found Monk difficult to play with. However, some had the temperament, technique, musical drives and caution necessary to work with Monk. Here are some of the best:

Steve Lacy

Steven Lackritz, known as Steve Lacy, was born in New York in 1934. Like his inspiration, the great saxophonist and clarinettist Sidney Bechet, Lacy became a virtuoso on the soprano saxophone (the 'straight horn'), cultivating a wide range of notes and considerable tonal purity. Lacy's music

tended towards subtlety, so he was well equipped to deal with the challenges of Monk's music, but, like Monk he was largely indifferent to the fireworks of bebop.

Lacy had a lengthy partnership with the free-playing pianist Cecil Taylor, sometimes called 'the Art Tatum of the avant-garde'. Following this, Lacy sought a more understated music which led him to Monk. He studied Monk's work obsessively, learning all his pieces and joining the pianist's band for a season in 1960. Lacy's high-pitched soprano sound was an ideal foil for Monk's dark, bumpy ruminations.

Johnny Griffin

In contrast to Lacy, tenor saxophonist Johnny Griffin embraced bop with open arms. A phenomenal improviser, with a reputation for the fastest negotiation of the idiom's shifting harmonies in the 1950s and 1960s, Griffin did not immediately seem to be an ideal partner for Monk. However, he was close in style to the blues and to the muscular, funky gospel music that had found a modernised jazz form in the 1950s 'hard bop' bands of Horace Silver and Art Blakey, of which Griffin was an early member.

Griffin was such a prodigy that he was on the road with the Lionel Hampton band as a 17-year-old in 1945, but in the late 1940s he spent considerable amounts of time with Monk and practised regularly

Soprano saxophonist Steve Lacy. With his sense of space, unusual melodic development based on thematic ideas rather than chords, and desire for jazz to move forward, he was a successful foil for Thelonious Monk.

with him. The relationship didn't publicly bear fruit for another decade. Griffin joined Monk's band in 1958 – having already worked in successful two-tenor partnerships with Wardell Gray, Dexter Gordon and Eddie 'Lockjaw' Davis. Griffin's explosive energy and speed supplied much of the tension and contrast in the group that Monk had found in his partnership with John Coltrane the previous year.

John Coltrane

This Carolina-born saxophonist was Monk's partner in the band that brought him back to public prominence in the late 1950s. Like Monk, Coltrane was reflective, retiring and obsessed with music and he shared Monk's preoccupation with questioning and extending accepted jazz styles. However his work had strength, urgency, and an appeal that extended beyond the usual jazz audience.

Coltrane was a member of Monk's quartet from July to December 1957, and the group became one of the short-lived legends of jazz for the empathy between its members and the rugged beauty of its music. Contractual difficulties restricted its recording opportunities, but on Blue Note's 'Live At The Five Spot', recorded on Coltrane's tape recorder, Monk's breaking-glass chords and hobbling runs still come forcefully through and Coltrane sounds much wilder than on the studio recordings.

Charles Rouse

Rouse was Monk's longest-serving musical partner. He played in the pianist's quartet from 1959 to 1970, almost all of Monk's later career. Rouse was not a spectacular technical master, but he had a distinctive, twangy tone, and an apparent indifference to solo stardom that enabled him to play in Monk's musical landscape. Like Monk, Rouse was rhythmically unpredictable and he mirrored Monk in manipulating repeated motifs. Rouse served a conventional bop apprenticeship, working in the bop bands of Billy Eckstine and Dizzy Gillespie in the 1940s, then with Tadd Dameron, Fats Navarro, briefly with the Duke Ellington and Count Basie ensembles, and with trumpeter Clifford Brown. After Monk's death, Rouse was joint leader of the Sphere quartet, devoted to the pianist's work.

Tenorist Johnny Griffin (above) was a harmony-based player who played very fast, yet his boppish improvisations had a crowded drive that contrasted effectively with Monk's minimalist style.

Art Blakey

Drummers often found Monk hard to work with because he was such a rhythmically-driven performer. However, Art Blakey heard Monk's message and shared his passion for the music of the black churches. Blakey founded the Jazz Messengers, one of the longest-lived and most famous bop bands, which included giants like Wayne Shorter and Wynton Marsalis. Bebop drumming could be dauntingly complex, but Blakey managed to provide a counterpoint to Monk's style, and punctuation that assisted the other soloists. Blakey's love of creativity gave him his respect for Monk, and made his bands ideal finishing schools for many jazz stars in the ascendancy.

3

Note Monk's flattened hand and splayed fingers. This unorthodox technique gave his music its percussive quality, and he played chords like a man striking a rock with a hammer.

This same year, a period when the pianist was also working with a Gillespie band on 52nd Street, Cootie Williams, one of the star trumpeters of the Duke Ellington Orchestra, also recorded a Monk original, the soon-to-be-legendary *Round Midnight*. The pianist's originality was beginning to be noticed, but hesitancy about his departures from swing and bop orthodoxies, as well as the American Federation of Musicians' recording ban of the mid-1940s, prevented Monk from recording under his own name for another three years. When he did, in 1947, it quickly became obvious that he had been brewing a startling confection of new work. This work later became appreciated as some of the most original and rigorously structured music of the 20th century.

Monk worked for the Blue Note record label between 1947 and 1952 and produced the miniature masterpieces that included 'Thelonious', 'Criss Cross', 'Evidence', 'In Walked Bud', 'Epistrophy', 'Straight No Chaser' and 'Misterioso', and in the process discovered in the restless Art Blakey a drummer who understood and could anticipate his personal sense of time. During the same period, Monk also worked as an accompanist for Charlie Parker, but in 1951 he was falsely convicted on a possession charge (the drugs were in a friend's car and Monk was the occupant) and as a result lost the vital police-issued 'cabaret card' that New

York entertainers had to have to work the nightclubs. To a jazz musician, for whom the majority of outlets at the time were nightclubs, this was tantamount to exile. Billie Holiday suffered the same fate in the early 1950s. James Lincoln Collier explains:

'The cabaret card had become infamous in the jazz world after Monk and Billie Holiday had their cards taken away from them because of drug convictions, and once they lost their cards they couldn't work in any place where liquor was sold. The whole idea then of the cabaret card was really quite a good one: it was to keep the gangsters out of the clubs. It wasn't aimed at musicians, it specifically was aimed at anyone who worked in clubs – waiters had to have it, bartenders had to have it, cooks had to have it, anybody who worked in a club. But New York City was the jazz capital of the world, New York City is the centre of showbusiness, New York City is where the press is, New York City is where the publicity is, so of course it hurt Monk not to be able to play in the clubs.

'But Thelonious Monk was playing music that was coming out of himself and I don't think his life circumstances affected what he was doing. He was doing what he was doing because he was Thelonious Monk, this is what he wanted to play, this was the kind of music he wanted to hear and that's what he did.'

In 1952 Monk was contracted to Prestige Records, a generally unsuitable relationship that neverthless produced classics like 'Little Rootie Tootie' (inspired by his son), an account of the Jerome Kern standard 'Smoke Gets In Your Eyes' that proved how effectively he could make familiar material sound both like itself, and also

'This work later became appreciated as some of the most original and rigorously structural music of the 20th century.'

3 THELONIOUS MONK

Thelonious Monk in Paris in 1966. By this time he was becoming more widely appreciated and even growing used to better hotels, better suits and better understanding from audiences.

like him, and a bad-tempered but productive session with the Miles Davis All Stars on Christmas Eve 1954. During this period, Monk also recorded with his long-time friend, saxophonist Sonny Rollins. But Monk's sales weren't impressing Prestige, and Orrin Keepnews acquired the pianist for Riverside, the jazz enthusiasts' label, where he remained for six years.

Keepnews maintains today:

'Monk was at Prestige for a couple of years and meant absolutely nothing to them. They had several very big selling jazz artists at that time, and they cared not at all for Thelonious who was difficult to work with, who didn't particularly sell and the word came to us that it might be very easy to get him out of that contract. He had been told by the owner of Prestige, Bob Weinstock, that if he repaid a specific over-advance that they had made to him they would release him from the contract. It was a hundred and twenty-seven dollars in change that he wanted from Thelonious, I personally lent him the money – even in those days it was an incredibly petty amount though it isn't quite as pitiful as it seems when you mention a figure like that today.

'The very first thing that we did . . . was to plan two albums, trio albums, no bebop horns in there, completely made up of standard tunes. Let's give people a shot at listening to Monk play tunes that they will recognize going in and it may be a little easier for them to understand him. So the first album we did to a very mixed reaction was the Ellington album. From then on, during the time he was with Riverside he was on a regular recording programme. The 'Brilliant Corners' album was very successful within the limitations of the jazz market, and he began to make a strong impact, so much so that when he was available to work again, this hip new Lower East Side Club, the Five Spot, was very anxious to bring him in.

'When he opened at the Five Spot, in a quartet with John Coltrane – and remember Coltrane had not yet made any impact on the world – it turned out that that was a wonderful thing and it was immediately evident to the the very hip New York audience that Coltrane with Monk was something special. The fact that more people were getting more of a chance to hear what he was doing, and perhaps just with the passage of time realised that it was very creative and not really that frightening, made that engagement, the roughly six months that they played at the Five Spot, the turning point.'

Monk in Paris, in 1964. This was the year Thelonious Monk made the cover of *Time* magazine - but celebrity status meant little to him.

Three Riverside albums – *Brilliant Corners*, *Thelonious Himself* and *Thelonious Monk with John Coltrane* – were high points of his career at that time. Following the Five Spot date, Monk began to run regular groups that included musicians such as the saxophonist Johnny Griffin, drummer Roy Haynes, and Charlie Rouse, the saxophonist whose style and thoughtful approach fitted better into the leader's demanding frameworks than many of his far more illustrious and virtuosic partners.

Monk began to tour regularly, at home and abroad. His pieces were arranged for full orchestras, rehearsed properly and played with dedicated attention. He moved to Columbia Records, and on to the cover of *Time* magazine in 1964, a rare accolade for jazz musicians. In

a rare concession to jazz salesmanship, Monk joined a showcase band, the Giants of Jazz, in 1971, touring with Dizzy Gillespie, trombonist Kai Winding, saxophonist Sonny Stitt, bassist Al McKibbon, and drummer Art Blakey. But although he made several triumphant appearances with an orchestra at Carnegie Hall, and was affectionately received by the Newport Jazz Festival audience in 1975 and 1976, Monk convinced himself he had said all he needed to. He withdrew from playing and recording, and spent his final years in seclusion in Weehawken, New Jersey, at the home of the jazz patroness Baroness de Koenigswarter, a lifelong friend whose Christian name, Pannonica, he had given to one of his grittily characteristic tunes.

4

CHAPTER

GERRY
MULLIGAN

'I think Gerry Mulligan never really thought of himself as part of the Cool movement. He wanted to play strong, driving jazz music and that's what he did.'

JAMES LINCOLN COLLIER, JAZZ HISTORIAN

Gerry Mulligan, the clean-cut, all-American jazz hero, was a walking definition of Cool. He helped bring modern jazz to the expanding student audiences of the 1950s.

Mulligan was a contradictory figure who was artistic but canny, who bucked trends and in the process spawned new ones, whose music was largely serene and whose temperament was anything but – and who began the ascent to his jazz stardom by breaking several familiar jazz moulds.

Firstly, Mulligan's chosen voice was one rarely used by jazz soloists, the deep-toned but rather lugubrious-sounding baritone sax, an orchestral ensemble instrument or a second horn for most saxophonists.

Secondly, at the crest of the first wave of the frenetic bebop era Mulligan was absorbed instead by music that was the diametric opposite – extensively arranged rather than improvised on perfunctory themes, and used European art-music instruments such as French horns and bass clarinets. In the 1950s, Mulligan's most famous small-group, although echoing bebop's language, left out the element that all the high priests of idiom thought crucial – the piano. But in the public mind, Mulligan was most notable for his pop-chart success, which he briefly enjoyed with the revolutionary piano less band – a rare event for postwar jazz of any kind.

Gerald Joseph Mulligan was born on 6 April 1927 in the Queens area of New York City. His father was an engineer, an occupation that kept the family constantly on the move, so the boy spent his youth in many places including Chicago, Ohio and Detroit. Mulligan later recounted that seeing the band bus for the popular Red Nichols Five Pennies in the street whilst on his way to school planted a dream of road-life and adventure that lasted throughout his career.

By the time he left school at 17, Mulligan, now living in the energetic music-city of Philadelphia, had been taught rudimentary piano, and – significantly, as his life turned out – some insight into arranging, by the dance-band musician who taught him clarinet. The teenage Mulligan got a job as an arranger, with the dance band of Tommy Tucker, an opportunity followed by a staff job at the Philadelphia radio station WCAU when he was just 17 – at which age he was also playing saxophone and clarinet professionally.

MOST OF THE FAMOUS movers and shakers of jazz gave the music new voices, usually by means of a familiar instrument, or a familiar format. The saxophonist and composer Gerry Mulligan went down a different road. For his achievements and charisma, Mulligan was awarded something close to star status in the 1950s, when he was associated with the legendary 'Cool School' of jazz. He was the model of a modern jazz musician of that era with his sharp dress sense, austere features, crewcut, shades and aura of brittle reserve.

THE BARITONE
SAXOPHONE

THE BARITONE SAX, like other saxophones, is a single-reed instrument from the family invented by Belgian instrument-maker Adolphe Sax, primarily for military-band use, around 1840. It has a conical wide-bore metal tube, and its tone-holes are controlled by sprung keys — a fingering system similar to an oboe. It is heavier and more cumbersome than the more widely used saxophones. Its wider column of air is heavier and so takes more physical effort to move, and playing it high or softly requires considerable technical skill and control of embouchure (application of the lips).

In the orchestras of the 1930s and 1940s, the baritone sax was usually the second instrument to an alto or tenor sax, and used sparingly to enrich an ensemble. But the Duke Ellington Orchestra, which had the resources to carry a five-saxophone section, and a musical approach that placed great emphasis on ensemble depth, featured Harry Carney, a powerful baritonist and a player with a rich sound and a romantic, shimmering vibrato. Carney was a model for aspiring baritone saxophonists, and others, such as Serge Chaloff and Cecil Payne, joined him from the ranks of the bebop players emerging in the 1940s.

During the 1950s, the emergence of Gerry Mulligan and the Swede, Lars Gullin, brought the instrument into greater prominence. The bop-influenced Pepper Adams was also a baritonist of speed, originality and agility, and John Coltrane's more free, impressionistic approach influenced post-1960s' baritonists such as John Surman, Charles Davis, and Hamiet Bluiett. Some of these musicians used strenuous and technically difficult overblowing techniques to release far higher ranges of notes than had previously been thought possible, taking the baritone within range of the tenor, or even the alto.

The baritone saxophone, the biggest sax in widespread jazz use, with its air column extended through considerably longer tubing at each end of the bore.

Gerry Mulligan (centre) on the set of the
1958 United Artists' movie *I Want to
Live*. Although rock'n'roll had arrived,
modern jazz still had cult status, a twilit
subculture often romanticised on screen.

But this was 1944, and the New York bop scene was beckoning to Mulligan, as it did to so many ambitious and adventurous young jazz players. In 1946 he went to work as an arranger for the drummer-bandleader Gene Krupa, for whom he wrote a popular swing tune, 'Disk Jockey Jump', that revealed his promise. The real focus of Mulligan's attention was the exciting world of bebop, and he joined the substantial number of young white jazz musicians orbiting in the comet-trail of Charlie Parker's genius during 1946 and 1947. However, by this time Mulligan was increasingly specialising in the baritone saxophone, performing with it in a bop group featuring trombonist Kai Winding, and softening its gutteral sound with the fragile, tenor-sax intonation of Lester Young.

The baritone saxophone presented Mulligan with certain technical challenges.

John Surman, the baritonist who hit the British jazz scene like a typhoon in the 1960s, says:

'You've got to blow the baritone hard, and when you do you get a very raucous sort of noise – so the difficult thing to do is to play it in a light way. Mulligan started out his career as a composer and arranger with Gene Krupa's band so he would have been listening to Charlie Ventura, who was quite interested in the baritone and played it rather well, but there were also coming up two key figures as far as the baritone saxophone was concerned, Serge Chaloff and Cecil Payne, players in the bebop style with lots of energy à la Charlie Parker. But Mulligan was particularly interested in that lean sound . . . using the upper register of the instrument in a very light way. If you look at Mulligan's face, he's got a very firm strong jaw line and lots of control over the instrument and that's what you really need, you need to be in control of the baritone otherwise it takes control of you.'

The seeds of 'cool jazz' were germinating in Mulligan's mind, a style quite different to hardcore bebop. Like the young white saxophonists Stan Getz, Zoot Sims and Jimmy Giuffre in Woody Herman's Orchestra, Mulligan's growing preference was for an improvising style with the fluency, displaced rhythmic emphasis and melodic unpredictability of bebop, but without its breakneck tempos, dynamic extremes, whistling high-notes and busy, domineering percussion. Like Charlie Parker, Mulligan and his close contemporaries were inspired by swing sax-poet Lester Young's way of phrasing a spontaneous melodic 'story', but unlike Parker they were less concerned with speed or distancing the music so far from the song chords that underlined it.

Mulligan found inspiration in his search for the right sound when he began working with Claude Thornhill's dance band in 1946. Thornhill, a classically trained pianist and arranger who had worked with Billie Holiday and Benny Goodman, originally formed his own band in

1940, and this was the second edition. Using instruments drawn from classical and jazz orchestras, the Thornhill band created a completely different setting for the improvisational experiments of the new jazz. Where Parker and Gillespie had envisaged stacked chords, bursting with augmented notes, unexpected key shifts, and furiously active percussion, the Thornhill orchestra was absorbed by chordal textures launched via unusual combinations of instruments, with a meditative, slowly unfolding quality that almost resembled drones. Claude Thornhill may have heard his music as a contemporary dance form of exquisite sophistication, but others, including Mulligan and Miles Davis, heard it as a challenge to a different kind of jazz improviser.

When Mulligan became involved with Thornhill's band he met a young Canadian arranger by the name of Gil Evans. Evans had educated himself in a wide range of large-ensemble approaches by meticulously studying the scoring for an immense variety of music, from Ellington to Beethoven. A coterie of young writers developed, involving Evans, Mulligan, and the ingenious self-taught trumpeter-composer Johnny Carisi. But, however absorbing their fantasies, composers need other musicians to bring their work to life. The Thornhill band, in its off-duty hours, became a composer's workshop. The beautiful chord movements and harmonies of the Thornhill band, an effect that came to be dubbed 'Clouds of Sound', attracted the 20-year-old Miles Davis and

another young white sax virtuoso associated with the Thornhill band, Lee Konitz. Today Konitz, now into his 70s, still exhibits a willingness to put himself into challenging playing situations, and work with unfamiliar musicians, that is almost unheard of for a player of his years in any area of music.

Konitz recalls:

'Miles Davis was a fan of the music and so we kind of all hung out together, and somehow I think through Gil Evans and Gerry Mulligan, they decided they would have a small Claude Thornhill band, with Miles playing the trumpet and being the titular head because he could get the gigs and get it recorded under his name. The objective was to have a chamber group where the good writers of that time, John Lewis, Johnny Carisi, George Russell, people who were really trying some new things with ensembles, had an opportunity. The soloing was part of the whole story, but basically it was a writer's workshop.'

The 'Birth of the Cool' sessions were crucial to Davis's early career, and they became a jazz legend. Mulligan later complained that his own role in the project had been obscured by Davis's subsequent stardom, and a perfunctory look at the scoring bears out his opinion. Five out of twelve cuts on that recording were Mulligan's, including 'Jeru' (Mulligan's nickname), 'Godchild', 'Venus de Milo', 'Rocker' and 'Darn that Dream'.

Although he was only 20 years old, Mulligan was interrogating the ground rules of Tin Pan Alley and the Broadway song form with simple questions. In the writing for 'Birth of the Cool', he was already experimenting with different measures, and different time signatures within the same theme. It gave the music a competely different feel from either bebop or the swing music that had preceded it. It was harder to predict where the melody was headed, how long it would sustain the feel of a particular phrase and how long it would muse on a counter-melody.

'It was harder to predict where the melody was headed, how long it would sustain the feel.'

THE
DANCE BANDS

THROUGHOUT THE CENTURY, the relationship between jazz and classical music has been uneasy. In the years before World War II, bandleaders such as Paul Whiteman and George Gershwin in the 1920s, 'Jazz Age', and Benny Goodman and Raymond Scott in the following decade, tried to bring the two disciplines closer together. Some of these attempts were successful, but in general they were forced matches, and sounded like it.

But by the 1940s, more of the musicians who were coming into jazz had some formal musical training and musicians began to wonder whether at least some classical-music techniques could be used in a jazz context and played by jazz musicians.

The white swing bands of Woody Herman and Boyd Raeburn were prominent in this movement, and their distinguishing feature over earlier incarnations of 'symphonic jazz' and of Swing itself, was that their melodic conception was increasingly overtaken by bebop. Dizzy Gillespie, pioneer of large-scale bop ensembles, wrote arrangements for his bandleading contemporaries in the 1940s, and even performed briefly in Boyd Raeburn's band. The episodic structure of some classical music, in movements with distinct identities, also appeared in their performances at this time. But if a stereotypically familiar gap was opening, between cerebral 'white' jazz thinking and intuitive 'black' perceptions, an unlikely ensemble emerged to bring the two together. The bandleader who unintentionally made the difference was

Claude Thornhill. Thornhill was born in Terre Haute, Indiana, in 1909 and studied classical music at the Cincinnati Conservatory and Philadelphia's Curtis Institute. He enjoyed a successful early career as an arranger for Paul Whiteman, Billie Holiday, Benny Goodman and others, and then formed a dance band – first in 1940, then again in 1946 when he returned from navy service.

Thornhill's music was influenced by Debussy as much as by any jazz inspiration. His music operated at a lower volume than the swing bands and used instrumentation that included French horns and woodwind. It was designed to be played in a more impressionistic manner than that of the hard-swinging, riff-driven ensembles of the jazz big-band circuit. He was a very experimental leader. Sometimes the whole reed section played the clarinet against the distant musing of the French horns, producing a haunting and poignant sound.

But the Thornhill orchestra's delicate methods were not really suitable to the dancefloor or for audiences accustomed to furious horn battles and wailing crescendos, and it was not a commercial success. However, Thornhill's main arranger Gil Evans used some of the band's methods to spark a very different kind of jazz revolution to the frenetic one of bop. Thornhill took over Evans' California-based band in 1938, and then Evans joined a larger Thornhill ensemble in 1941.

Evans described the Thornhill ensemble as a 'cloud' of sound, and this approach to jazz ensemble-writing fascinated many musicians, although the public was largely indifferent to

it. Thornhill and Evans' work was crucial to what became known as the 'Birth of the Cool' experiments at the end of the 1940s. Although little of the Thornhill band's music survives on record, a few radio transcriptions indicate how good the music really was. Thornhill soloists in the mid-1940s included the young altoist Lee Konitz, and trumpeter Red Rodney (who was to join Charlie Parker). Claude Thornhill's career was affected by a breakdown and heavy drinking in the 1950s, though he continued to run dance bands. He died in 1965.

The influential Claude Thornhill Orchestra in 1941. Primarily a dance band, but a very sophisticated one, its ensemble sound was adopted by the Cool School pioneers.

Gerry Mulligan, c. 1958. The big baritone saxophone hardly seemed a suitable instrument for the light sound and melodic agility that Mulligan was taking from Lester Young and Charlie Parker, but in his hands it worked.

As Lee Konitz points out the 'Birth of the Cool' band was shortlived:

'The band had a very short history. We rehearsed some and recorded a few days and played one of two weeks, as I recall. The band was hired for two weeks at the Royal Roost Club at that time, played one week, but didn't do the two full weeks. It didn't sound that great. Changes in personnel, and not much opportunity to rehearse, and it was very delicate music. The final version on the records is less than perfect, and it's always amazing to me that it had such a long life. But the quality of the music was, of course, what kept it alive.'

Mulligan's name became widely known at the sharper end of the jazz world. He financed his self-imposed apprenticeship as an arranger by continuing to work for Thornhill in that capacity, and also for bandleader Elliot Lawrence. But, although Mulligan recorded for the Prestige label in 1951, he was largely inactive except as a commercial arranger during the years following the Birth of the Cool sessions, and a drug habit increased the pressures on him both psychologically and financially.

Searching for a way out, Mulligan hit the road in the early 1950s. He hitched across the United States from east to west, picking up gigs on the way, and wound up in Los Angeles, working for Stan Kenton, the ambitious, often adventurous bandleader whose blends of jazz and classical music were appealing to a new audience for jazz in the expanding postwar college population. Mulligan and the Kenton musicians frequented a variety of local nightclubs, including The Haig, a converted bungalow on Wilshire Boulevard that was pushed to accommodate an audience of 80, or any band much bigger than a quartet.

The club's publicity was handled by Richard Bock, who later became boss of Pacific Records, the most significant West Coast jazz label. The Monday night session attracted most of the up-and-coming younger musicians, including trumpeter Ernie Royal, fiery alto saxophonist Sonny Criss, pianist Jimmy Rowles and drummer Chico Hamilton. In 1952, the young trumpeter, Chesney 'Chet' Baker visited The Haig club. His talents had been noticed by Charlie Parker shortly before.

Mulligan and Baker began playing together once a week, on The Haig's Monday-night session. They shared a mutual desire for a more ambiguous and understated music than bebop, and they found that with a softer attack, a more even group dynamic and a considered approach to the quantity of notes, they were developing a form of muted bop that had its own kind of lyricism, as well as a harmonic subtlety that suggested the input of more musicians than were actually present. In June 1952, Bock began recording the group. When, at a later session, Rowles and the drummer Chico Hamilton didn't show up, Chet Baker stepped in.

Mulligan and Baker's tunes were usually taken at a relaxed mid-tempo rather than New York bebop's downhill slalom, and Mulligan's baritone sax, pitched in a deeper register, offered more 'orchestral' possibilities than a tenor or alto sax would have done. Significantly this music, although its phrasing and melodies suggested bebop, also appealed to those who complained that 'modern' jazz was unmelodic, wasn't danceable and had sacrificed its heart to its technique. The cool, James Deans of the new white-bop West Coast movement would have been mortified at the thought that they were appealing to the disaffected jazz fans who were

'They were developing a form of muted bop that had its own kind of lyricism.'

GERRY MULLIGAN

THE BIRTH OF THE COOL

T HE 'BIRTH OF THE COOL' sessions have become part of jazz legend. Gil Evans, Gerry Mulligan, trumpeter/ arranger John Carisi and Dizzy Gillespie pianist John Lewis were the original architects of the recordings, although the sessions actually went out under Miles Davis's name, as he was the best-known and most bankable of the group. Evans had an apartment near Times Square in New York where musicians would frequently assemble, particularly members of the Claude Thornhill band, and it was here that 'Cool Jazz' was born.

The agenda for these informal composers'-workshops was to balance the economic constraints on a small group against the desire to recreate the Thornhill sound as a backdrop for improvisers. This unique sound was described by historian James Lincoln Collier as 'like Debussy sung in a cathedral'. Evans, Carisi, Mulligan and Lewis worked on adaptations of the Thornhill sound, and the resulting band, named after its primary soloist, became the Miles Davis Nonet. The instrumentation of French horn, trumpet, trombone, tuba, alto and baritone sax, piano, bass and drums raised many eyebrows in the jazz world.

The band played a largely unsatisfactory two-week engagement at New York's Royal Roost club. There wasn't time for adequate rehearsal, and the calm, unfolding momentum the group desired was only fitfully achieved. It might have folded completely, but a Capitol Records' enthusiast heard the band recorded it between January 1949 and March 1950. Four of the arrangements were by Mulligan, the rest by Evans, Carisi, Lewis, and Davis. Gerry Mulligan's 'Jeru' was typical of the group's bold departure from more usual jazz forms. 'Cool Jazz' would often operate in two contrasting tempos, the sound-levels were mostly muted, and the standard bar structures of conventional jazz vehicles were often stretched or squeezed, a particular challenge to the improvising habits of soloists.

It was the collection of the Nonet's recordings onto an album, named 'Birth of the Cool', that put these events into the perspective their innovations deserved. Miles Davis went on to become a jazz legend and, from the late 1950s to the 1980s, Gil Evans became one of the best-loved figures in jazz.

Evans' energy and awareness of evolving contemporary musical developments won him almost every kind of accolade and balanced his ensembles between composition and improvisation. An Evans band sounded as if it were improvising even when playing written ensemble parts, the result of the leader's openness to the contributions of players. This also imparted a sense unfolding musical drama to the group's performances that could never be accurately notated. The Cool School continued to pursue the aims of more restrained playing, cushioned ensemble parts, and Europeanised art-music feel after the short-lived Davis-Evans experiment with the Nonet, and although the public was generally uninterested in its more ascetic and mathematical investigations (although the contrapuntal Mulligan/Baker band was popular), groups of mostly white musicians on both coasts continued to explore a more understated brand of bop. Pianist Lennie Tristano, with saxophonists including Lee Konitz and Warne Marsh pursued the idea in New York. And on the West Coast, pianist Dave Brubeck proved, as Mulligan and Baker had, that the public's heads could be turned if the mixture was accessible enough. Brubeck was a student of classical composer Darius Milhaud, and his alto saxophonist Paul Desmond was a delicate improviser. Brubeck was intrigued by rhythmic manipulation, and his pieces varied the regular metres of bop – so much so that the tune 'Take Five', in 5/4 time, became a major chart hit.

The other best-known practitioners of the Cool ethos in the late 1950s and into the 1960s were the Modern Jazz Quartet. Originally formed from Dizzy Gillespie's rhythm section, and including the sophisticated and subtle pianist/composer John Lewis, a devotee of baroque music as well as jazz, the MJQ developed an intricate, tiptoeing kind of bluesy bebop, strongly featuring the vibraharp of the great Milt Jackson.

also supporting the concurrent Dixieland revivalist trend, but their ensemble-based, conversational, lightly-swinging music tapped a younger audience's desire for a more lyrical, more easily followed jazz.

Mulligan avoided using The Haig's poor piano for the Monday-night jams so Chet Baker, Mulligan, bassist Bob Whitlock and drummer Chico Hamilton thus formed a pianoless quartet, and Bock quickly concluded that it had potential, and set up a new label – Pacific Jazz – to record it. Mulligan's arranger's ear gave him confidence in the notion that the contrasting horns and double-bass would imply chords, as long as they agreed on the tonal centre and listened to each other, and the bass played a central role in sustaining the harmonic movement. In August 1952, Bock recorded the quartet playing 'Bernie's Tune' and 'Lullaby of the Leaves', and the band was a chart hit within months of the record's release.

Lee Konitz reflects on Mulligan's bold stratagem in abandoning the piano:

'It's possible to have a little more freedom without it. As I'm playing my melody, trying to put my melody together, I hear this sound (of the piano) and though I have an idea there's a certain given information on a given tune, and there's supposed to be this kind of a sound, but I don't know how the pianist is going to choose to arrange the notes, and I don't know if he's going to choose to put another chord there instead of the one that is traditionally there.

'So I go . . . diddle diddle dee. And then I hear the chord he decides to play, and I have to go . . . diddle diddle diddle, and go maybe in a different direction. We've referred to the piano players and the chordal instruments as switchboard joes. They're sitting there and guiding us in some way. Either we allude to them in some remote way or try to leave enough room to really hear and be affected by the sound they're making, and then that makes it possible to get some kind of dialogue going.'

Bill Crow was periodically Gerry Mulligan's bassist from 1956 to 1965. He maintains Mulligan heard the bass line

Mulligan (right) was a good improviser, but he heard music in the same way as an arranger.

occupying a more prominent role than many arrangers did, and often built the piece of music around it.

Crow asserts:

'A lot of times he would think of the bass line first, and his melodies would grow out of that. It was a kind of arranging technique that he used that worked very well even though it was only four people he was arranging for, and one of them was a drummer. One of the things that made that group so attractive was that they did play a lot of standards that people knew, but were able to tweak your ear a little different way about the treatment.

'The bass keeps the rhythm moving the same way the drummer does but also lays down an indication of the harmonic line without spelling out every chord, and with that foundation Gerry was able to take other notes of the chord when he wasn't soloing and make little accompanying melodies, little lines that also implied the harmony and would give a richer background for the soloist to play on.'

Chet Baker (left) and Gerry Mulligan in the recording studio, 1958. Between them they defined the Cool sound for a wide audience, and even had chart hits.

Bill Crow says:

'The reason it ("My Funny Valentine") was a hit was because Gerry was fortunate to have Chet's voice there. Chet was a very lyrical player, got a beautiful sound, and he knew how to just phrase a melody so that it drew you through it and gave it some emotional meaning.'

Yet for all the delicacy that gave the band its unique sound and touched such a deep chord in the public, those qualities were often conspicuous by their absence under Mulligan's leadership offstage. Bill Crow laughs when he recalls what working for Mulligan could be like:

'Oh, he was an ego maniac. But very likable. I think that was part of what gave him that star quality, that made it possible for the rest of us to work. He was able to organise his music and his relationship of . . . himself as a player and a bandleader to his audiences in a way that most of us didn't really know how to do. I think a lot of that came out of his egocentricity.'

Was he always striving for perfection?

'In others. No, that's a joke. But he set a different standard for himself. I mean, he was good, he could really play well and he really knew what he was talking about when he talked about music, but sometimes he tried to hold his musicians to a higher standard of dedication to his music than he held himself. He used to drive me crazy sometimes, but in retrospect I must say that without Gerry I probably wouldn't have learned as much about music as I did.'

After the success of 'My Funny Valentine' more recording sessions followed quickly, as Bock sought to take

Mulligan and Baker's soft, subtle outfit often sounded as if it was blowing smoke rings rather than notes, and suggested classic Broadway songs being sung quietly, coupled with the precision and fragility of a classical chamber group. News of the group spread up the West Coast. When they appeared at the Blackhawk club in San Francisco pianist Dave Brubeck recommended them to the Fantasy record label, and 'Line for Lyons' (after Jimmy Lyons, who later produced the Monterey Jazz Festivals), 'Bark for Barksdale', the Latin dance tune 'Carioca' and 'My Funny Valentine' were recorded. The latter was an instant hit, and the setting for Baker's horn playing (walking bass, distant vocal choruses, then Mulligan's haunting sax) made the solo improvisation and the ensemble sound dovetail perfectly.

'. . . he was an ego maniac. But very likable. I think that was part of what gave him that star quality . . .' BILL CROW

CHET BAKER &
LEE KONITZ

Chet Baker, the classic jazz anti-hero –
damaged, strung-out, lost to all but music.
But beneath the romantic bohemian
mythologising, he could be a brilliant
improviser, in song as well as on trumpet.

I F A SINGLE INDIVIDUAL symbolised the white 'cool school' of jazz in the 1950s it was Chesney 'Chet' Baker. Baker was the James Dean of jazz in the pre-rock era, when his mixture of rebellious youthfulness, soft trumpet sound and crooner's voice were at their best. An icon of doomed youth, he eventually succumbed to heroin addiction, but he was also an intuitive trumpet improviser, an imaginative interpreter of fast bop, and one of Miles Davis's most creative descendants. In his cool tone, and in his lifestyle, Baker was in some respects the modern Bix Beiderbecke.

Baker was first noticed by Charlie Parker on the West Coast, and shot to celebrity status with the success of Gerry Mulligan's pianoless quartet, formed at The Haig in Los Angeles. For much of the 1960s and 1970s, Baker was silenced by drug problems, and the performances he gave were often aimless and confused. However, in later years he gave many remarkable performances. His trumpet sound and his singing voice sounded bruised, but although both could be unsteady in pitch, their sound could be expressive enough to appeal to jazz and non-jazz audiences alike.

The Chicago-born alto saxophonist Lee Konitz has also regularly partnered Mulligan, and, as he enters his 70s, he is still playing with curiosity and imagination. He has become the best-known survivor of the original 'cool school' and his solos are recognisable for their mix of scurrying runs, indignant hoots, breathy low notes, languorous, flute-like ascents and sustained sounds wreathed in long silences. His primary influence was the Chicago pianist, teacher and theoretician Lennie Tristano, who disliked jazz's dependence on standard song-forms and excessive volume. Konitz also worked with Claude Thornhill, on the 'Birth of the Cool' sessions with Mulligan's 1950s groups, and with the gifted tenor saxophonist, Warne Marsh, with whom his contrapuntal improvisation seemed all but psychic.

GERRY MULLIGAN

advantage of an unexpected overnight sensation. Mulligan tunes like 'Soft Shoe' and 'Walkin' Shoes' joined the band's quickly expanding book of catchy original themes. Bill Crow analyses the band's secret:

> 'Putting the harmonic role entirely in the hands of the bass player was revolutionary. Nobody was doing it, everybody was going in the other direction giving everything very explicitly. So by implying the chord structure, by just hearing the bass walking through the harmonies and having one of the two horns who wasn't soloing to step back and play little lines that wound around the harmonies like that . . . those kind of innovations are interesting.'

Lee Konitz sometimes augmented the first quartet on alto sax, and his intelligence and acute listening powers that rivalled Mulligan's enabled him to fit into this intimate new format as if he had played in it since its inception. He reflects:

> 'Of course, counterpoint wasn't exactly new, Johann Sebastian Bach was doing it three hundred years ago, . . . and the nature of his melodies was very akin to the kind of melodies that we liked to play. Very continuous melodies of sixteenth notes, very rhythmical music, not very impressionistic in the use of the materials, just really swinging, and I think that was a great influence to all of us . . . two melodies or more can exist at the same time if they're strong melodies. They don't necessarily have to meet along the way.'

Bill Crow adds:

> 'It's like stringing beads. At the same time each person is aware of how his line is crossing the other person's line, imitating it, mirroring it, going counter to it, whatever, but they always stay within the sound of the harmony. Gerry was a good listener and I don't remember ever working with anyone who was more aware of what I was playing behind him. He was not so wrapped up in his own playing that he didn't hear

what everybody else was doing. But it used to drive him crazy in noisy rooms that he's playing this music and there are people who aren't listening, and he would take them to task about it quite often, he was very good at lecturing his audience. But he liked the freedom of playing in nightclubs because of the lack of pressure in those situations, where you had maybe four sets in a relaxed circumstance where he could try a lot of things.'

Throughout 1953, the quartet went from strength to strength. More sessions for Fantasy followed and there were personnel changes as Carson Smith, Bob Whitlock's regular deputy came in permanently, and drummer Chico Hamilton was replaced by Larry Bunker. Jazz historian James Lincoln Collier reflects on the group's unexpected success with the public:

> 'Gerry Mulligan was a genius at figuring out accompanying lines, and when you listen to that quartet, with Baker playing an improvisation and Mulligan playing very simple but beautifully constructed lines behind it, this was a kind of music that people could grasp, it was first-rate jazz, uncompromising jazz, but it was relatively simple . . . Mulligan and Chet Baker were young, they were good looking, they looked hip, they were very easy to package but it was the music that counted really, and the music was accessible – great jazz but accessible and so people bought it.'

As well as steering the group's direction through his own compositions and astute choice of standards, Mulligan was also aware that being a bandleader was in part an act of salesmanship. The detailed, sometimes obsessive attention he gave to all aspects of the job was also

reflected in his musicians' appearance onstage – a preoccupation that continued through all the later incarnations of his groups.

Bill Crow recalls that:

'Gerry was always conscious of how we looked on stage. We were in Boston one time, and we went out to the Andover shop, which was a chic little mens' store that the college guys all went to. We each picked out a sport's coat and slacks in a different fabric but in the same general style so that we'd look sharp on stage. Another time it was hot weather, we were playing a lot of festivals in the summer time in tents and things, and Gerry took us down to a little boutique on Sixth Avenue where the dancers go, and bought us red and white striped short-sleeved shirts and sky blue trousers that were very tight – we looked like American flags – and little black string ties. Dizzy (Gillespie) loved that. He said, "Oh, look at these fools". Gerry liked the slender clothes that were in at that time, Ivy League suits where they took the pads out of the shoulders and added a button to the jackets,

A group of Cool Jazz stars at Newport in 1957. Mulligan (left) is on baritone, with Jimmy Giuffre on tenor next to him. Jim Hall, an exquisite guitarist, is seated.

slender pipe-stem legs, all that. And he changed his hairstyle regularly and grew beards and shaved them off, went through a Christ-like look for a while, then a very closely barbered military look. He was always trying things out.'

In the summer of 1953, Mulligan's narcotics problem resulted in his arrest and a three-month prison sentence – ironically at a time when he was trying to break the habit. He emerged to find Baker seeking to treble his wages in the light of the quartet's earlier success with the public and in the jazz polls. Mulligan's refusal meant the end of the group and his return to New York, and the emergence of Baker as a leader of his own sessions.

SYMPHONIC JAZZ
COOL STYLE

As PAUL WHITEMAN HAD FOUND twenty years before, there could be a paradox about increasing the level the organisation along European classical lines without clipping the wings of a jazz band's greatest asset, its improvisers. Gerry Mulligan's Concert Band of his later career trod that line very successfully, and although the leader's compositional subtleties were always evident, he would vary the spaces left open for soloists according to how they felt on the night, and encourage supporting musicians to adapt and extend written accompanying parts according to the heat of the moment too.

During the 1940s, the great Duke Ellington led the field at this difficult art. His band's pieces were complex and richly textured, yet the special qualities were intimately woven into them – so the purring sound of saxophonist Ben Webster, the cry of trumpeter Cootie Williams or the driving beat of pioneering virtuoso bassist Jimmy Blanton would be indivisible from the overall impact. As adventurous composer/ arrangers with a profound understanding of improvisation, artists like Gerry Mulligan and Gil Evans were inevitably influenced by Ellington's bluesy tone-poetry, but also by the quicksilver mechanics of bebop, and a growing enthusiasm – particularly among white musicians, but also in the black Modern Jazz Quartet – for links with classical music. Several other bandleaders were investigating the same possibilities in the late 1940s and into the 1950s, through the jazz-classical music marriage proved a difficult relationship to sustain.

Stan Kenton

As well as the Claude Thornhill Band and its jazzier offspring, the Miles Davis Nonet, there were a number of ensembles that were exploring these avenues in the late 1940s and into the 1950s. Wichita-born Stan Kenton was one of the most commercially successful and widely admired bandleaders of the time. Influenced by Stravinsky and Ravel, Kenton's music, although innovative, was later criticised for hyperbole and affectation, and his performances were often very loud and complex, sometimes using up to 40 players.

In the late 1940s, Kenton dedicated himself to what he called 'progressive jazz', experimenting with dissonance and mixed tempos. but commercial concerns forced him back to a more conventional perception of jazz in 1952, and, with fine soloists including trombonist Frank Rosolino and saxophonists Lee Konitz and Art Pepper, he built a substantial following, particularly on the college circuit. As his performing career waned, Kenton developed an alternative career as a coach and talent-scout for budding musicians on American college campuses.

Gerry Mulligan's hard-swinging arrangements of Kenton favourites like 'Young Blood' and 'Swing House' were among some of the best in any postwar big-band's repertoire.

Woody Herman

Kenton's major rival through this period was bandleader Woody Herman. Herman had originally been a vaudeville child star on clarinet, and he stayed on the road relentlessly through his life, took over his own orchestra at 23, and sold a million copies of his pre-war hit, 'Woodchoppers' Ball'. After the war, Herman formed the first of his famous Herds, creative combinations of swing and bebop methods, with a significant smattering of classical music's vocabulary thrown in. Igor Stravinsky even composed a piece for the Herman band, called 'Ebony Concerto'. Star Herman soloists included the young saxophonists Stan Getz and Zoot Sims, musicians who, like Gerry Mulligan, were suspended between the innovations of Charlie Parker and the earlier, more lyrical saxophone style of Lester Young. Herman's chief arrangers, Ralph Burns and Neal Hefti, did much to make the Herman bands the powerful force they were, and revealed that the arranger's craft was just as important to jazz in the post-bebop world as it had been in the Swing Age.

The Stan Kenton Band in Los Angeles. Kenton dedicated himself to what he called 'progressive jazz' and believed that the jazz tradition and the European art-music tradition could come together. His bands were often exciting, but the results of the merge of musical styles were mixed.

With Baker gone, Mulligan brought in Bob Brookmeyer, a trombonist who played the valve-operated version of the instrument. This achieved a quick delivery but a rounded sound that effectively compensated for the lack of a trumpeter, even if fronting two low-voiced instruments compacted the tonal range of the band. Live recordings of the band, notably Vogue's Paris series from the 1954 Salon du Jazz festival, prove that Brookmeyer's mellow sound and elegant execution was a fitting but independent replacement for Baker.

Mulligan returned to California in 1954, and this time his group featured a new trumpeter, Jon Eardley. Eardley had a steady, composed feel as an improviser and a luxuriant sound, and was equally at home with ballads or the group's understated swing. Mulligan was also writing regularly for a ten-piece rehearsal band at The Haig, an outfit that bore close resemblance to the 'Birth of the Cool' band. But following relatively few appearances with the reshaped quartet, Mulligan abandoned California for New York at the end of 1954. His reputation now ranged far beyond the West-Coast jazz scene, and he consistently dominated the jazz polls as a baritone saxophonist.

Frustration with the lack of opportunities to develop his rare talent for large-scale work, and some spare cash from movie-score work, led Mulligan to organise a 13-piece group, the Concert Jazz Band, in 1960. Bill Crow, who regularly worked in the Concert Band says:

'Gerry called it the Concert Jazz Band because he wanted to play concerts. He wanted the focus to be on the music, he wanted people to come and listen in the same way they would listen to chamber music. We had good riff-makers in every section so we would never go onto the next written section until Gerry gave us the signal because Willie Dennis might be playing a solo on trombone and Gerry might start to play a little background like he used to with the quartet, and immediately the rest of the saxophone section would harmonise what he was doing and then Bob Brookmeyer might think of some answering figure that the brass section might play, and it would go on maybe for another ten choruses before we could get onto the next written part. That would keep the arrangements very alive from night to night, you never knew exactly what was going to happen. So they kept it much more with the kind of freedom that you have with a quartet or a sextet. Gerry told us when he was first putting the band together that he didn't want this to be a screaming band. At the softer level you could hear all the inside parts and it stays more rich. It's also easier on everybody's chops.'

The Concert Band toured Europe and Japan, although a downturn in Mulligan's fortunes later in the 1960s led to more extensive work as a freelance arranger and as a sideman in other leader's groups, notably pianist Dave Brubeck's. The support of jazz impresario Norman Granz had looked promising for the Concert Band for a while, but eventually the outlets declined to a handful of appearances at clubs like New York's Birdland, a few college dates and recordings, interspersed with long layoffs, and eventually Mulligan had to call it a day. He came back to the idea a decade later however, in 1972, with a 14-piece band called The Age Of Steam (reflecting an enthusiasm for steam railways that went back to his Pennsylvania childhood). He was also artist-in-residence at Miami University in 1974, ran a sextet that included vibraphone-player Dave Samuels, and took up soprano saxophone. As the climate swung back toward a renewed public enthusiasm for America's great jazz innovations in the 1980s, and the irascible *enfant terrible* of the Cool School years turned into something of an elder statesman, new opportunities came – even for a 20-piece big band. In the mid-1980s he also resumed small-group work, forming a quintet with the mainstream tenor-sax star Scott Hamilton. As widespread respect for classic jazz extended into record company investment, Gerry Mulligan was able to reform the Birth of The Cool instrumentation – a project that might even have featured Miles Davis's trumpet, but was forestalled by Davis's death in 1991.

Jazz Historian James Lincoln Collier says:

'I think Gerry Mulligan never really thought of himself as part of the Cool movement, I think he saw himself as a hot jazz player, he wanted to play strong, driving jazz music and that's what he did. Mulligan and some of the others saw this whole notion of Cool as an invention, which it basically was, a record company hype and they didn't want to be categorised by it.'

Like Miles Davis, Gerry Mulligan was a forceful, demanding and sometimes petulant artist whose impact on the bands he worked in was the precise opposite — selfless, encouraging of ensemble equality, preoccupied with the evolving form of a group improvisation rather than the reputation of a star soloist, taking the longer view that the pressures of jazz improvisation and jazz economics sometimes obscure.

John Surman says:

'In some of the jazz groups at that time you've got a *mélange*, a wash of sound. In Gerry Mulligan's bands you can very clearly pick out the different voices, and I think that's the joy of listening to that group in its different forms through the years. He had one or two different front-line partners playing with him, but in all cases you could hear the distinctive voice of each of them.'

Gerry Mulligan became an elder statesman of jazz in his later years, bringing to new audiences the elegant swing and lyricism of his musical youth. He disliked the 'Cool' tag, but his attempt to re-form the Birth of the Cool band with its original trumpeter was only forestalled by Miles Davis' death in 1991.

5 CHAPTER

ELLA
FITZGERALD

'Ella was the gold standard,
she brought the whole idea
of pop singing as well as jazz
singing to a different level.
You had to be almost dead not
to love what she was doing.'

GARY GIDDINS, JAZZ CRITIC

Ella Fitzgerald seemed to find singing as natural as talking. Some say she sang like an angel and some like a child, but she made the most taxing technical feats sound easy.

ELLA FITZGERALD WAS one of the greatest of all jazz vocalists. Some say that she sang like an angel, and some say like a child. But although both descriptions fit, she sang most like someone who found singing as natural as speech, making beautiful music as simply as if she were accompanying some everyday activity. Privately, however, Ella Fitzgerald was not the exuberant figure she appeared to be on stage. She was rarely at ease with either her talent or her appearance, and even though her name was known to millions, her deeper feelings were hardly revealed to the public at all throughout a long career.

Fitzgerald's effortless-seeming performances were the product of her astonishing vocal technique, as flexible, wide-ranging and accurate as any of the greatest jazz instrumentalists, and with an inbuilt swing that was as propulsive as the most hard-driving drummer. It was the combination of her buoyant optimism, and her apparent naivety that made her a jubilant jazz communicator throughout a career that ran at full throttle into her 70s.

Fitzgerald had her first hit when she was 21 with the song 'A Tisket, A Tasket', and throughout her career she won the admiration of musicians, especially singers, from every musical genre and included Frank Sinatra, Peggy Lee and Elton John among her devoted fans.

Singer Dee Dee Bridgewater, who in 1997 released a disc devoted to Fitzgerald's achievement entitled simply 'Dear Ella', says of her:

'Ella Fitzgerald . . . the original definition of a jazz singer for me. Omnipresent. Of all jazz singers it's Ella Fitzgerald's voice that has come to be associated with what we term jazz singing today. And it's the name that is known all over the world.'

Village Voice jazz critic Gary Giddins puts it this way:

'Ella was the gold standard, she brought the whole idea of pop singing as well as jazz singing to a different level. You had to be almost dead not to love what she was doing.'

And pianist Tommy Flanagan, Fitzgerald's regular accompanist for many years, says:

'Her ear was just about perfect, and she grasped songs and the material quickly. She had been doing this all of her life by the time I got there, so the pressure was on me, and not on her.'

Ella Fitzgerald was the daughter of William Fitzgerald and Temperance ('Tempie') Williams, Fitzgerald's common-law wife. She never knew her father, who

THE
BOSWELL SISTERS

Two strands of singing fed the jazz music of the swing era. The blues was an African-American remix of hymn forms and communal singing that emerged out of the American south. The other, Tin Pan Alley, emerged in New York from a tradition of songwriting, often the work of east-European Jewish immigrants with rich traditions of folk and popular song. After the First World War, these elements mingled with the jazz music from the Southlands. Ethel Waters was the first show singer to develop this tradition and was the inspiration to many singers of the day, black and white, among them the New Orleans-born Boswell Sisters.

Connee, Martha and Helvetia Boswell were white sisters born in New Orleans. The Boswells blended their vocal sounds with fluent ease, and as their work developed, the arrangements became more complex. Connee, the most skilled and subtle of the three, also played saxophone, trombone and piano.

In the 1930s the Boswell Sisters became international celebrities and successful recording artists, particularly with the highly successful Dorsey brothers – and their singing style became the foundation for the work of many close-harmony clones, notably the Andrews Sisters in the United States and the Beverley Sisters in Britain. Connee Boswell was the star of the trio, and although she was not an improviser in the traditional instrumental jazz sense, her propulsive swing and sense of timing were admired by many jazz musicians, and she exhibited deeper emotion than many big-band vocalists of the day. Poliomyelitis made her wheelchair-bound for much of her life, but she nevertheless began a career as a solo artist in 1935 and sympathetically interpreted songs from many genres. She worked steadily until the 1950s, appearing in several movies and touring frequently. Her public appearances tailed off in the 1950s, but she made a highly regarded mainstream-jazz album with a band including trombonist Miff Mole in 1956. She died in New York in 1976.

The Boswell Sisters were the most popular close-harmony singing group of the 1930s, and although they didn't sing jazz, their fluency and skill influenced jazz vocalists.

THE
HARLEM DANCE SCENE

THE INFLUENCE OF Africa on western dancefloors in the 20th century has been as important as its influence on music. From the 'slow drag' of New Orleans brothels, to the shimmies and shuffles that became, with a little help from jazz, the Charleston, the Black Bottom, the Lindy-hop and the Suzy-Q, a freer, more expressive, more overtly sexual form of dancing began to replace earlier, more formal styles.

In New York, this development was part of a much wider social change that accelerated the cultural traffic between white and black life. Although both casual and institutional racism remained endemic for decades to come, a fascination with the history and traditions of the African-American population became fashionable in upmarket East Coast white circles in the 1920s. This search for new inspiration may have been triggered by the traumatising of traditional western values in the First World War. Black Americans politicised by the effects of racism in army life, and by the ghettos of the industrialised north to which they had migrated, also sought a celebration of black achievement and history and the result was 'the Harlem Renaissance'.

This flowering of black American visual art, poetry, literature and thought also pollinated the dancefloor via Broadway musicals such as *Shuffle Along* and *Runnin' Wild* in the early 1920s. The dancing in these shows was sensational, and the latter production launched the Charleston, which became a cult around the world. Bill 'Bojangles' Robinson and Earl 'Snakehips' Tucker (the latter a particular favourite with the young Ella Fitzgerald) astonished audiences in the 1928 hit production *Blackbirds*, and nightclubs and ballrooms in New York's Harlem became a focus for young black and white audiences alike. Duke Ellington's famous residency at the Cotton Club from 1927 to 1931 produced such classics as 'Black and Tan Fantasy',

tone-poems ostensibly satisfying the desire of a liberal, white audience for imagery of the simple and spiritual life of the black community, but which themselves became permanent edifices of early jazz.

And so the swing era began. In around 1930, when Ella Fitzgerald was old enough to catch the train from Yonkers to Harlem with her friends, the New York music scene was on a sensational roll. American dance-music was reaching an unprecedented level of vibrant sophistication. Although successful classically orientated white bandleaders like Paul Whiteman had forged a reputation with an elegant blend of jazz and the European symphonic music for upmarket dance-floors, the lasting impact was being made by bands in which the jazz content was far hotter.

Arrangers Fletcher Henderson and Don Redman developed an ensemble sound in which the vocalised tonality, raw attack and complex inner rhythms of the New Orleans jazz soloists like Louis Armstrong and Sidney Bechet was being orchestrated for groups of players. The effect instantly redoubled both the refinement and the excitement.

The Wall Street Crash of 1929 had a crippling effect on the entertainment business, particularly on recordings that were made specifically for black audiences, as the black community was the hardest hit financially by the Depression. But jazz bands playing for dancers survived, and Henderson and Redman's prototype for a new dance orchestra sound – a strong jazz flavour allied to multi-layered arrangement and a smoother, more flowing underlying four-beat groove – lit the fuse for the explosion of big-band jazz that occurred around 1935. Unsurprisingly, the biggest beneficiary was a white band, clarinettist Benny Goodman's. It appealed both to a larger and more affluent social group and was resoundingly kicked onto the jazz stage by the newly-expanded national

Jazz and dance have developed hand in hand: in Harlem, dance-hall bands would
play for ecstatic crowds. In the 1930s, the beat became smoother, the volume
louder, and the excitement hotter. Dancing was Ella Fitzgerald's first love.

radio network. But the popularity of the Goodman band, and of the Dorsey Brothers and Artie Shaw, was mirrored by the ecstatic reaction to black orchestras in the black dancehalls such as Chick Webb's, Duke Ellington's and Count Basie's by the mid 1930s. At huge establishments like New York's Roseland or Savoy, orchestras would play flat out for most of the night, on revolving stages that wasted no time setting up between one band winding up and another coming on. Often the bands played 'cutting contests' or 'band battles' in which the audience's enthusiasm would determine who had played loudest, fastest and most inventively that night. This was the era of jazz as mass-market pop music. There has never been an era like it since.

ELLA FITZGERALD

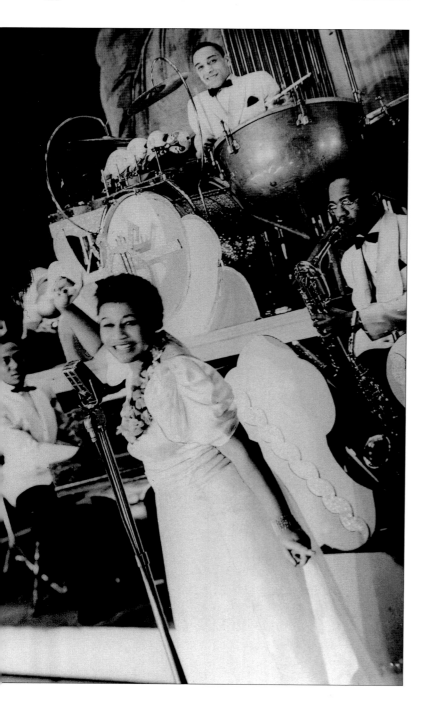

Ella Fitzgerald at the age of eighteen, with Chick Webb (drums). She lacked confidence and doubted both her appearance and her singing, but Webb encouraged her to stardom.

appears to have died not long after her birth, and she moved with her mother to Yonkers, north of New York City. Tempie quickly found herself a new partner and not long afterwards Ella found herself with a half-sister. It was, according to Fitzgerald's own accounts, a happy childhood and a warm and affectionate home, and the street-sharp eccentricities of the locality were part of everyday life. At eight she was acting as a lookout for local prostitutes, and being a runner for the 'numbers game', collecting bets from the neighbours. Most of her schoolfriends were Italian and the area was racially mixed, but Fitzgerald reported hearing no racial abuse until she was called 'nigger' by a new kid in school when she was 11. Her popularity soared when she flattened the boy for that comment.

Her ear for music quickly revealed itself, and for a while she had piano lessons. At home she heard the popular singers of the day on the gramophone, and her mother liked female close-harmony groups like the popular Boswell Sisters. Ella also listened to the radio, and her accurate imitations of the pop singers of the day (mostly white) added to her popularity at school. But she also liked the sound of Louis Armstrong's smoky singing voice, and could mimic that style too. The combination of her love of open-handed popular song, uncanny mimicry, and a grasp of jazz intonation and swing – were crucial to Fitzgerald's development, and her popularity.

She was also a fine dancer, and dancing was her first love. The connection between dance and jazz was booming, and the nightlife of Harlem was a magnet for a clientele – not simply drawn from the city's black youth, but also from an upscale white audience who were attracted by the vivacity of a subculture that in the late 1920s came to be known as 'the Harlem Renaissance'. From their early teens Fitzgerald and her friends regularly took the train to Harlem to visit, among other places, the Savoy Ballroom on Lenox Avenue – the biggest and most glamorous dance venue in the district. New dance crazes followed on each other's heels. The Suzy-Q and the Lindy Hop were hugely popular, as were the idiosyncratic dance styles of soloists like Earl

'Snakehips' Tucker, whose upper and lower body appeared to function completely separately. Fitzgerald could do an impressive imitation of Tucker, and by her early teens she was able to dance on the streets for cash.

The Harlem ballrooms ran amateur nights, which Fitzgerald and her friends often discussed entering. In 1933, when she was 15 years old, Ella entered a contest at the Harlem Opera House, as a solo dancer. But when her turn came to dance, stagefright paralysed her. Unable to move, she sang instead. The words of Connee Boswell's 'Judy' surfaced, the orchestra recognised it, and Fitzgerald and the audience warmed to each other. By the end of the song they were cheering, and she continued with Boswell's 'The Object of My Affections'. Moments before, they nearly had to push her onstage, now she had to be reminded that her time was up, and she realised that this was the future she wanted.

Long before this, Fitzgerald had sought refuge from her anxieties in entertaining others, but now she found that a bigger audience could love her too. She entered more amateur contests, often with the Boswell Sisters' repertoire, and although the occasional hitch reminded her that singing on stage wasn't always easy, her clarity and growing command of her material put her in the premier league of amateur contenders. But this was still a long way from Connee Boswell's life. Fitzgerald needed someone with more clout than ballroom MCs and the audience to notice that she had arrived.

One night in 1934 at the Apollo Ballroom, the saxophonist and bandleader Benny Carter heard Fitzgerald sing. Carter knew how to distinguish a showbiz performance from a musical one, however raw. When he heard Fitzgerald, he realised that he was hearing something unique. Carter later said that it was her simplicity as well as her remarkable range and

Ella Fitzgerald (right) with Duke Ellington (foreground) at Harlem's famous Savoy Ballroom in 1938. A decade before, Ellington had been impressed by Ella's mentor, Chick Webb – and his endorsement helped secure Webb's crucial residency at the Savoy in 1933.

accuracy that had impressed him. He recommended her to the influential white jazz impresario John Hammond, who arranged an audition with the star, black bandleader Fletcher Henderson (one of the architects of the Swing Era, and later a great influence on the successful Benny Goodman Orchestra). Henderson disliked Ella's preoccupation with white pop styles and didn't hire her, but shortly afterwards she was offered a contract for regular appearances on a CBS radio show called 'The Street Singer'. It felt like the break she was waiting for. But disaster struck when Tempie, Ella's beloved mother, who had been a constant source of encouragement and steadying advice, died suddenly.

Ella, now living with her half-sister and her aunt, Virginia Williams, dropped out of school, and the tough Harlem streets became her classroom once more. In February 1935, when

'When her turn came, stagefright paralysed her. Unable to dance she sang instead.'

CHICK
WEBB

Baltimore-born William Henry 'Chick' Webb was one of the most dynamic and entertaining bandleaders of the swing era. The energy he imparted to his bands from the drum chair often gave them the edge on more obviously skilful or sophisticated orchestras, even including Duke Ellington's. But his rise to a brief celebrity status in the world of the jazz ballrooms was a considerable triumph over adversity. Webb

had suffered tuberculosis of the spine as a child. He was diminutive and hunchbacked, but took up the drums at a doctor's suggestion to develop what strength he had, sold newspapers on the streets to raise money for his own drumkit, and was a self-taught virtuoso by the age of 15.

Although Webb was barely able to read or write, his memory for musical arrangements was astonishing – he rarely needed to hear a piece of music more than once to play it fluently, and this talent endeared him to Duke Ellington, who arranged a first job for Webb's young Harlem Stompers band at the Black Bottom Club in New York in 1926. Webb's star continued to rise as the Swing Age dawned, and although his bands frequently went through changes of personnel (the hold Webb maintained over his colleagues on captivating musical grounds was often overcome by economic pressures) it was a Webb orchestra that eventually won a coveted residency at Harlem's legendary Savoy Ballroom in 1933.

Because of his disability, Webb found combining the roles of drummer and front-man difficult, so singer and conductor Bardu Ali dealt with the public relations. However, Webb was intimately involved with musical policy. Promoter George Wein, architect of the Newport Jazz Festivals, said that 'Chick Webb was probably the most intensely involved with music of any jazz musician who ever lived'.

By 1935, the Webb band had become one of the most popular draws in Harlem. Webb foregrounded his own drumming much more. He also relished the 'band battles' that were a regular feature in the ballrooms – even Duke Ellington sometimes suffered at Webb's hands and said 'everybody in the band played like mad at all times'. But by the late 1930s Webb's health was hampering his playing. During a 1939 tour to promote Ella Fitzgerald's hit 'A Tisket, A Tasket', he was hospitalised in Baltimore, and died on June 16.

Bandleader Chick Webb, Ella's mentor, in the late 1930s. A thrilling self-taught drummer, the disabled Webb was only a child's height, and the pedals of his kit were specially adapted for him.

she was 16, Fitzgerald made her professional debut at the Harlem Opera House, on a bill headed by the Tiny Bradshaw Orchestra. Bradshaw part-funded a dress for the newcomer, who had nothing to wear for such a high-profile assignment. She completed her first week's work as a singer wearing it.

Singers became popular with the development of radio, and bandleaders saw that they could appeal to live audiences. Whether or not they added musical quality, girl vocalists could be sexy and appealing. Fitzgerald broke onto the swing scene as this transformation was well underway. But she needed a mentor who understood the business, and had her best interests at heart to help her overcome her self-doubt, stagefright, unworldliness and loneliness. Fortunately one was coming – Chick Webb.

William Henry 'Chick' Webb hardly seemed like a gallant protector. He was little more than four feet in height, the result of childhood tuberculosis of the spine and a subsequent serious fall. He took up drums as a muscle-strengthening activity on doctor's advice and was a virtuoso by the age of 15, despite needing built-up pedals to play. He was encouraged by Duke Ellington and led his own band two years later. Webb had become one of the big draws among the Savoy Ballroom's regular swingbands, when he heard about Fitzgerald.

Webb had a male singer, Charlie Linton, and at first was unwilling to engage a female one. But when Fitzgerald was brought to Webb's dressing-room by Webb's front-man and conductor Bardu Ali, to audition with 'The Object of My Affection', the drummer got the point at once, exactly as Benny Carter had done, and took her on.

Fitzgerald was homely-looking, disconcertingly timid and had clothes no woman in the entertainment business would go to the corner-store in, let alone wear to stand in the footlights. Many influential men in the business were not initially convinced of Ella's potential. Bardu Ali and Webb therefore subsidised Ella Fitzgerald's wages on her early gigs with them because promoters would not

'She needed a mentor who understood the business, and had her best interests at heart.'

consider paying for her. But one influential man was definitely in Webb and Ali's corner: Charles Buchanan, the Savoy Ballroom's manager. Between them, the men paid Ella's wages, and bought her some clothes, and at the end of a third week at the Savoy singing with Webb's band, she had become a fully paid-up staff member.

By sheer talent, Fitzgerald rose above an abiding prejudice. James Lincoln Collier tells 'an old jazz story':

'There's a jazz musician who dies and ends up meeting St Peter, and St Peter says, "Well, you can go to heaven or you can go to hell. Right here in heaven we have Charlie Parker, we have Bix Beiderbecke, we have Benny Goodman, we have all the greats, and you can play with these guys". The jazz musician says, "You mean I can come and play with Bix and Charlie Parker?" St Peter says, "Sure". So the jazz musician says, "Well, why wouldn't I want to do that?" St Peter says, "Well, there's one thing, the Boss has this chick who thinks she can sing".

'Now that's an old story, and the kind of story that jazz musicians tell about girl singers as they were called then. But in fact there were many, many wonderful singers and musicians loved to play with Billie Holiday, Helen Forest who was a quintessential big band singer, and they loved to play with Ella.'

Fitzgerald's natural musicianship succeeded where her personal marketing skills failed. Life on the road with the Webb band was not her ideal environment, and she was polite but distant with the musicians – but since she was shy and unglamorous, they left her alone and she left them alone. Webb and his wife became Ella's legal guardians, and the bandleader nursed his protégée's contribution, conscious of her youth and vulnerability. At first she rarely sang more than a couple of choruses at

Ella in 1954. Technical developments in the electric microphone by this stage enabled vocalists to compete with the roar of a big band at full blast while also allowing them to be quiet and confiding in the huge Harlem ballrooms.

his beat could wake the dead. She and the Webb band became nationally famous through a string of sensational shows at the Savoy Ballroom, and through late-night radio broadcasts and recordings. The mid-1930s were the boom years of Swing and the new craze was heavily dependent on radio. Webb secured his own 30-minute slot on NBC in 1936: 'The Gems of Colour'. Fitzgerald was almost uniquely qualified to reach a wider audience and broaden her appeal because racial divides in the marketing of 1930s pop music were very marked.

Writer Will Friedwald, a specialist in jazz singers says:

'There was a very small period in the beginning when she was considered a race artist, even before Chick Webb. I think that what Chick Webb realised was that here was a way for his band to break through, beyond just playing for the black audience but to the big audience beyond . . . Some people say that Ella Fitzgerald sounded white. When people say that I have to say, define a white sound. But she does not sound like a Mississippi blues singer, and blues is not one of her strengths. She has a sound which is not racially distinct in any way I would say. She does not have, what we would tend to think of as a black sound or a blues sound or a southern sound. It's just a perfect mid-American sound.'

a time, and always on up-tempo numbers rather than emotionally demanding ballads. As an untrained singer, her breath control and pacing left a lot to be desired, but the teachers Webb considered using concluded, with consoling enlightenment, that her natural talent was best left to itself. Fitzgerald however, took a modest view of her prospects. She considered her singing 'hollering'.

Fitzgerald said Webb always taught her to follow the beat, and Webb's regular followers were convinced that

In early 1938, whilst on tour in Boston, Webb was taken to hospital with one of recurring bouts of tuberculosis. The band continued without him, and during a rehearsal for a radio broadcast in the city, Ella Fitzgerald began musing with a children's rhyme, and she and arranger Van Alexander turned it into the novelty song 'A Tisket, A Tasket'. Fitzgerald took the lyric, as she later said 'from that old drop-the-handkerchief game I played from six to seven years old on up'. When she sang it in front of the

THE
MICROPHONE

HE STARS OF THE 1920s' blues and vaudeville circuit, like the formidable, operatic Bessie Smith, were as familiar with bold projection and dramatic volume as classical singers. However most jazz and popular vocalists preferred to work in more intimate ways. The microphone was part of a revolution in sound reproduction that affected not just the jazz world, but also the movies, radio and recording.

Microphones made it possible to capture a human voice in all but its entirety – and allow the subtlest nuances to rise above the sound of a drumkit, or other amplified instruments. In search of ever more accuracy, engineers in the recording studio moved from dependence on a single, central microphone, with the quietest instruments closest, to the contemporary set-up in which the drummer alone may have a dozen microphones placed around the kit.

In live shows, singers began to get close to the emotions of their audiences when even lowering their volume to a whisper against a full orchestra. The sound of an indrawn breath, a sigh, a delicate elision of pitch could be crystal clear to every member of a packed house, and a different kind of popular singer emerged – capable of conveying the more ironic, downbeat, personal and idiosyncratic materials of the rising composers of Broadway musicals, like George Gershwin, the Berlin brothers, or Harold Arlen.

The high priest of the new 'crooners' was Bing Crosby, who established a previously unimaginable intimacy between singer and listener. Crosby was close to the 1930s jazz world, as was an even more celebrated successor, Frank Sinatra. Billie Holiday, the most subtle and oblique of all jazz vocalists, possessed a small, fragile voice that might never have brought her international stardom without the invention of the microphone. Peggy Lee, whose career took off in front of Benny Goodman's 1930s' orchestra, was a soft singer with rich overtones to her voice, using the microphone to float above the roar of the brass.

Ella Fitzgerald in Hamburg in 1954. The battery of microphones are for radio stations – the invention not only made the subtlest nuances of jazz singers audible and improved recording, it also permitted the radio transmission, often live, that helped the jazz story to spread.

band, the audience adored it. So a week after her 20th birthday, Ella Fitzgerald recorded the song for Decca. It became a huge commercial hit, and spent 17 weeks in the pop charts, selling over a million copies. It became the most requested song in the Webb band's book and led to her recording other novelties such as 'Melinda the Mousie' and 'I Got Me A Pebble In My Shoe'. Will Friedwald explains the enduring popularity of mundane Fitzgerald material:

> 'The reason those records are still great and they're still worth listening to is because of Ella and the quality of the band. She could just sing anything.'

'. . . Webb's regular followers were convinced that his beat could wake the dead.'

Blue Note's Michael Cuscuna develops the theme:

> 'This was an era when people made their living by performing live, not from record royalties. Let us not forget that in Ella's case, 'A Tisket, A Tasket' is something that she wrote herself. So we can't blame commercial forces for making her sing the song. It was something of her own devices. That was a necessary evil in those days, and a very important one. You could go into the recorded canon of almost any singer – Nat Cole, Dinah Washington, Billie Holiday – and you'll find some of those in there. Everyone has to pay the rent.'

In June 1939, Webb was persuaded, despite worsening health, to take the band on tour to promote Fitzgerald and 'A Tisket, A Tasket'. But he was taken to hospital early in the tour, the band continuing with a replacement drummer. On 16 June news came through that the bandleader had finally bowed out. 'I'm sorry, I gotta go' were Webb's departing words.

There was little time to absorb the shock – Fitzgerald became one of the youngest big-band leaders in the world at 21, as well as one of very few women in such a

Ella Fitzgerald recorded many pop songs in the 1930s and '40s that would have fallen by the wayside but for her unique treatment. She put heart and enthusiasm into everything she did.

position. Still shy and deferential, it was not a role she exploited, and Bardu Ali took over practical control. But she worked tirelessly, in the recording studio as much as on the road. Much of the material was junk, but it didn't matter. There was always enough to remind the more attentive listener that a unique creative spirit was growing. Her success and talent also presented her with opportunities she had once believed nature had denied her – in romance. With Webb gone, Fitzgerald sought protection in the brittle early years of the war by marrying a dock-worker and sometime dancer called Benny Kornegay. But the marriage was quickly dissolved, and in later years Fitzgerald never discussed it – except to suggest that she had embarked on it for a dare.

She continued to work for Decca Records, often under the direction of producer Milt Gabler, and the material was largely directed toward the pop charts. During the 1940s, as the popularity of swing and the big bands waned, her hit-making talents appeared to be deserting her. But a brief partnership with the successful vocal harmony quintet, The Ink Spots, was popular on live shows in late 1943, and the following year produced the million-seller 'Into Each Life Some Rain Must Fall'. 'I'm Beginning to See The Light' also sold a million in 1945.

Fitzgerald fronted Dizzy Gillespie's bebop-oriented orchestra for two years, a manoeuvre organised by the agency that represented them both. It was a significant step, Gillespie's orchestra was attempting a marriage between a fast-moving, highly spontaneous small-band music of melodic hairpin-turns (bebop) and a music of less restless and abrupt changes of direction, closer to pop-song familiarity (big-band swing). The experience

Norman Granz (right) changed Ella Fitzgerald's career. He believed she was stuck with the wrong material and that she could be a peerless interpreter of the Great American Songbook of classics by Gershwin, Arlen and Berlin.

British vocalist Anita Wardell says:

'It sounds easier than it really is. There's a lot of homework that you have to do, you have to know what's going on underneath, so that you can follow this with your ear – treat scat-singing like an instrumentalist. Ella's the Queen of Quotes in my opinion. She borrows sounds from the Boswell Sisters, and then she'll imitate instrument sounds, you'll get the bass, and then she'll go right up to the high range and imitate a trumpet sound she's borrowed from Dizzy Gillespie.'

American singer Dee Dee Bridgewater recalls the impact of Ella Fitzgerald at full throttle in live performance:

'I was completely mesmerised. She just sang and sang and sang. She sang, like, twenty-four songs in two hours. You just got so caught up in watching her and also maybe, it had to do with that little girl sound, that quality that she had to her voice that made her so appealing. She also had a very large vocabulary in terms of the actual syllables that she would use . . . and an innate sense of timing, like a singing metronome.'

widened Fitzgerald's knowldege. Her astonishing retentive musical memory had captured and stored dozens of melodic spins and turns from Chick Webb's instrumentalists, and she did the same with Gillespie's players, who played faster, and more intricately. She loved working with Gillespie, and was later to say: 'I used to just get thrilled listening to them.'

Technically able to take the melodic convolutions and unpredictable switchbacks of bop phrasing in her stride, she made a successful and influential recording of the swing tune 'Flying Home' in 1945. Scat-singing, or the improvisation of wordless, instrument-imitating lyrics, originated from Louis Armstrong's engaging manipulations in the 1920s but Fitzgerald took it much further. Today's jazz singers remain in awe of the technique she developed in those years.

In December 1947, Fitzgerald married Gillespie's virtuoso bass player Ray Brown, a musician who was following in the footsteps of men like Duke Ellington's Jimmy Blanton in developing an agile, horn-like vocabulary for the double-bass. Fitzgerald and Brown adopted a son they called Ray Jnr. But Brown was considerably younger than Fitzgerald, and both were highly successful musicians in their own right, with professional agendas of their own to pursue and the contradictions destabilised the marriage. In 1952, Ray Brown moved out of the house in Queens they had bought three years before, and divorce quickly followed.

The big bands always struggled economically after the war, but Fitzgerald's career soon moved on, partly as a result of Fitzgerald's own strengths, but also because of a fundamental change in the role of vocalists in pop music. James Lincoln Collier explains:

'The singers became more popular than the bandleaders – Frank Sinatra, or Perry Como became the draw rather than the band itself. Eventually club owners said, "well what do we need to hire the whole band for, we'll hire the singer, get a trio, and we can get the whole thing cheaper." That happened with Ella Fitzgerald of course.'

Many kinds of music were closely related at this time. 'Jump music', a blend of jazz and up-tempo blues, was a popular style and the forerunner of rock 'n' roll. Much of this music was targeted at black audiences. But some black artists, like Nat King Cole, bridged the gap between the intonation and delivery of African-American music and the more urbane forms of pop music that appealed to white buyers. In concentrating on the products of Tin Pan Alley, Fitzgerald unintentionally brought together the creativity of white Jewish East European immigrants like the Gershwins and Irving Berlin with her own roots in the black ballrooms of Harlem.

Fitzgerald also worked in a small-group with the young Canadian piano virtuoso Oscar Peterson on Granz's *Jazz At the Philharmonic* shows in 1951. This was

'She does not have what we would tend to think of as a black sound . . .'

WILL FRIEDWALD

an important step as she adjusted to a changing musical climate that was freezing out the big bands, and the affable Peterson helped her to cultivate a more easygoing stage presence at the same time.

As her confidence grew, she left the Gales and Glaser agency she had been associated with since the early days, and Norman Granz became her full-time adviser and manager – an occasionally turbulent but mostly beneficial

A meeting of giants – Ella Fitzgerald with Nat 'King' Cole at the Paramount Theatre in New York. Cole was a brilliant jazz pianist but it was his singing that made him a star.

JAZZ
DIVAS

IF THERE WERE TWO galvanising influences on the art of jazz singing in the period before the swing boom, they were Louis Armstrong and Ethel Waters. Louis Armstrong sang as if his trumpet and his voice were interchangeable. His voice slurred one note into another and the emphases against the underlying beat and unpredictable placing of the rhythmic patterns created an absorbing tension in the sound.

Eventually he became principal innovator of the 'scat' style of singing in which the voice mimicked the sound and phrasing of musical instruments. Ethel Waters was a cabaret and show singer with a less idiosyncratic style and fewer explicit references to jazz than Armstrong. However, she perfected an informal, intimate, relaxed delivery that was capable of bringing singers and audiences much closer together.

Billie Holiday, 'Lady Day'. Where Ella Fitzgerald was fast and instrument-like, Holiday could be achingly restrained, far more influenced by blues, and delay the beat to give a languorous, sensual feel.

When the folk-blues roots of 19th-century black America, the ragtime-based jazz of the Southlands, and the upmarket notated dance music of the metropolitan centres travelled separate roads, these strands in American music impinged little on each other. But with the dawn of the 1930s and the beginning of the Swing Age, they met. To make their jazz enthusiasms more acceptable to general audiences, and to handle requests for the popular songs of the day, the orchestras all featured vocalists. Many barely coped, or were present for their personalities or their physical attributes only. But some were clearly as musical as the instrumentalists who laid out lustrous ensemble carpets for their voices. The great jazz divas, who held sway from the 1930s to the 1970s and rose alongside Ella Fitzgerald, all emerged from the swing era. The experience, and the exposure to constant musical invention in a climate that (however tightly organised) still depended crucially on improvisers, showed in everything they did.

Billie Holiday (1915-1959)

Billie Holiday was Ella Fitzgerald's closest contemporary, influenced by Harlem club-life at much the same time. But where Fitzgerald's sound was pure and clear, Holiday's was smokier and more rhythmically audacious – she would often hang provocatively behind the beat to give the music a sensual, world-weary air. Like Fitzgerald, Holiday was under Louis Armstrong's spell, but she was more absorbed by the blues, and her early female model was more often Bessie Smith than Connee Boswell. An intimate and delicate performer of exquisite timing and control of nuance (the newly-developed microphone technology might have been made for her), Holiday worked better with small groups than big bands, and her partnerships with the saxophonist Lester Young and pianist Teddy Wilson are among the vocal classics of jazz. Billie Holiday was marketed as a victim figure in the 1950s, a development that her habits with narcotics and alcohol hardly dispelled. But there was a gritty strength and defiance, even bruised buoyancy, about her music to the end of her life – and although the famous anti-racism song 'Strange Fruit' made her a postwar success with a bigger audience, it was not typical of her output, nor really representative of her astonishing facility for conjuring music of fascinating complexity and ambiguity out of the most apparently minimalist materials.

Sarah Vaughan (1924–1990)

Sarah Vaughan was a singer of the opposite style, perhaps the closest phenomenon to an opera star the first five decades of jazz was to see. Vaughan had a four-octave voice, and could soar to a trumpet-section's roar, or drop to the whisper of a flute. She had begun as a church singer and, like Fitzgerald, won a Harlem talent contest with 'Body and Soul' when she was 16. Stepping on to the jazz stage at the beginning of the 1940s, Vaughan's concept was inevitably shaped as much by bebop as swing, however, and she worked with Charlie Parker, Dizzy Gillespie, white 'cool school' pianist Lennie Tristano, and the famous prototype bebop orchestra of singer Billy Eckstine. Augmenting a superb natural musical ear, Vaughan was also highly knowledgeable musically – like her contemporaries Dinah Washington and Carmen McRae – and a capable pianist with a good understanding of harmony, and the input showed in the unpredictability of her phrasing.

Sarah Vaughan's abilities consistently broadened throughout the 1950s, as she moved away from the romantic repertoire that had bought her success and towards a taut, jazzy format with minimal accompaniment that simply showcased her dazzling tonal scope, rhythmic relaxation (possibly even more apparently effortless than Fitzgerald's) and bursts of sheer power.

relationship. Sure that Fitzgerald's sound belonged on a bigger stage than the one usually commanded by jazz artists, Granz pushed hard to open new doors for her – including exclusive clubs like Hollywood's Mocambo, where she delivered a one-off show to an audience that included Marilyn Monroe and Frank Sinatra and was such a hit that she was retained for a season. Fitzgerald was also warmly reviewed for her part as Hard-Hearted Hannah in the Hollywood movie 'Pete Kelly's Blues'.

In 1955 and 1956 Ella Fitzgerald's and Norman Granz's relationship was also frequently augmented by the presence of lawyers. Together, they successfully sued

'. . . she was so good every singer wanted to be like her.'

GARY GIDDINS

Pan-American Airways on a racial discrimination case after Fitzgerald and two other black musicians had been forced off a Pan-Am plane en route to Australia in 1954. Granz also managed to wriggle the singer out of her Decca contract by suggesting that he might otherwise withhold permission for some of his artists to appear in *The Benny Goodman Story*, which was made by Decca's parent company, Universal Pictures. He promptly formed the Verve Records label to showcase her, and thus the most significant phase of Ella Fitzgerald's career began.

She now directed her genius toward a succession of powerful reinterpretations of works of great American songwriters. The Songbooks series embraced Jerome Kern, Cole Porter, Rodgers and Hart, Irving Berlin, Duke Ellington, Johnny Mercer, Harold Arlen and Frank Loesser and extended the Gershwin project that had begun it. The albums brought Grammy Awards, new venues and new audiences. By the end of the 1950s she was a success with jazz and non-jazz audiences throughout the world.

Blue Note record producer Michael Cuscuna says:

'The idea of a Songbook as an expanded project was really making use of the LP as a 40-minute delivery system, for the first time. As a concept from beginning to end. Now concept albums are commonplace and they've played actually in a far more important part in pop music than they have in jazz. But I think this was the first real instance of something that was meticulously and thematically set out, to accomplish a concept larger than a series of cuts strung together. In that sense it not only served her well but it probably upgraded the targets that people were setting for themselves in this new era of the LP'.

But if Fitzgerald's career under Granz's guidance had been virtually relaunched from the recording studio, she still remained a thrilling live performer, and a variety of live recordings (most notably 'Mack the Knife' from 'Ella in Berlin') confirmed how surefooted, how musical, yet how consistently spontaneous and fresh her appeal to audiences remained. By the 1960s she was touring up to 45 weeks a year, a punishing schedule that led to her collapse onstage in 1965. She also began to develop eyesight problems and diabetes from the early 1970s.

Despite declining health Fitzgerald continued to perform and record into the early 1990s, broadcasting on occasion with Frank Sinatra, performing with symphony orchestras, small-groups, and at times Count Basie's tirelessly swinging band. Privately, she regretted to friends some of the choices she had made in life partners, remained shy and guarded throughout her later life, living in Beverly Hills and seeing only a small circle of friends, many of whom were musicians, including

Carmen McRae and Peggy Lee. *Downbeat* magazine named her best female jazz singer for 18 consecutive years, and she received awards and doctorates from all over the world. 'Not bad for someone who only studied music to get that half credit at high school' she once said. In 1987, she received the National Medal of Arts from President Reagan, one of her most valued tributes.

Ella Fitzgerald's work was not always a favourite with jazz fans – many disliked singers on principle, or preferred to hear a more pungent flavour of the blues than she ever delivered. But today, and with a hindsight that increasingly puts the musical developments of this century in perspective, music-lovers are almost unanimous in astonished gratitude to Fitzgerald's achievements. The *Village Voice's* Gary Giddins says:

'Ella Fitzgerald was an innovator in the sense that she was so good every singer wanted to be like her . . . She had everything, impeccable taste, she could sing a Cole Porter tune and make it completely convincing, and she could turn around and do a scat vocal on a Lionel Hampton riff and be just as convincing. She had great humour, suddenly in the middle of a scat performance like 'Mack The Knife', she could be terribly witty and full of ebullience, and so every singer just idolised her'.

Dee Dee Bridgewater puts Fitzgerald's gift in perspective against the reservations about her emotional depth:

'We all suffer. Ella suffered in her life. She was sometimes distraught when she was not able to be with her son, she had health problems, she suffered racism, she was a very courageous woman. But she hid her suffering. Ella was a bright person and she tried to project joy and a kind of lightness with her music.

By the late 1960s, when this photograph was taken, Ella Fitzgerald was touring up to 45 weeks a year. The routine was punishing, but she loved singing and loved audiences. *Downbeat* magazine named her best female jazz singer for 18 consecutive years.

Billie Holiday was caught up in her life, the bad experiences that she'd lived came out through her music, her voice was more transparent in that way. Ella was able to mask it. But still I think that the reason why she sang like she did was out of her suffering. That was the one moment where she could forget everything and be this beatiful flower, be this beautiful human being. You know, I look at her sometimes, and think she must not have thought that she was such an attractive woman. But she realised she had this amazing voice. That was her gift. The stage was where she felt magnificent'.

WES
MONTGOMERY

6 CHAPTER

WES
MONTGOMERY

'He was just a natural, you
know. It seemed like nothing
he played could be wrong.'

TOMMY FLANAGAN, JAZZ PIANIST

A close-up of Wes Montgomery's right hand would be enough to tell guitarists who was playing – this bebop guitar sensation plucked with his thumb instead of a pick, which gave him a uniquely soft, singing sound.

Like many gifted creators, Montgomery made what he did seem effortless. He possessed the improviser's ability to play virtually anything that he could think – although the way he amiably surveyed his audience as streams of notes spun from his fingers deceptively implied that conscious thought played little part. He plucked the strings with his thumb rather than with a plectrum – and the ensuing softened sound was warmly expressive and optimistic. Because of this quality of openness, Montgomery was able to reach beyond the jazz cognoscenti to a wider audience, with his later albums becoming easy-listening bestsellers. Although his evolution split his loyal fans. But countless guitarists have adapted or copied him, and still do.

One of Montgomery's most celebrated followers is George Benson, the Pittsburgh-born musician who has enjoyed two separate musical careers – one as a jazz guitarist carrying on Montgomery's tradition in legendary late-night jams, the other as a soul singer with a string of hits, including the chart-busting 'Breezin' in 1976. Benson has never made any secret of Wes Montgomery's shaping influence on his career:

'Montgomery came about all of us. Meaning, all the players had to turn around and see who this incredible player was, because he was coming from a different angle, a different point of view. The harmonic concepts were pretty basic, but the way that he used them were more akin to the piano than they were to saxophones and trumpets. His tone was magnificent because he played without the pick. Montgomery was unique from all those points of view. He was a great musician. His approach to the single line and harmony was just nothing short of amazing, the way that he got around the instrument was completely unheard of before.'

F ROM THE VERY beginnings of jazz music, wind instruments have mimicked all the perfections and imperfections of the human voice. Where Louis Armstrong's voice ended, and his trumpet sound began, seemed at times like an unnecessary distinction to draw.

The guitar has been constrained by design from making such an impact, although in rock and pop, musicians have found an expressive eloquence. But as modern jazz developed from the late 1930s, the guitar became more accepted as a solo instrument. One name is still mentioned with awe by contemporary players in this context, even though it belongs to a musician who died almost 30 years ago: it is Wes Montgomery.

DJANGO REINHARDT

EUROPE MADE LITTLE IMPACT on the consciousness of American jazz musicians before the World War II, but one European musician, the Belgian gypsy guitarist Django Reinhardt, was recognised as an improvising genius even in the birthplace of jazz. A romantic player with a singing, violin-like tone, Reinhardt had an intuitive understanding of harmony. His capacity for spontaneous invention at any tempo allowed long sustained flights without repetition, his sensitivity to contrast and pacing was composer-like, and his rhythmic sense made his solos constantly surprising. Reinhardt could execute trills like a pianist, was a moving player of ballads, and occasionally used a method of building melody based on octaves rather than on single notes, a technique adapted by Wes Montgomery.

He was born in Charleroi, Belgium, on 23 January 1910 and died at Fontainebleau, France, on 16 May 1953. The son of a gypsy entertainer, he learned the violin and guitar as a child, but lost the use of two fingers of his left hand in a caravan fire and was forced to abandon the violin. He developed a guitar technique better than that of all the jazz guitarists of the day. He learned the music of Louis Armstrong, Duke Ellington, and violinist Joe Venuti from records, worked in dance bands during the early 1930s, and helped found the legendary Quintet du Hot Club de France in 1934, with violinist Stephane Grappelli – an ensemble that attracted the best, including American tenor-sax king Coleman Hawkins.

The Quintet caught the imagination of jazz lovers everywhere and, although its life was shortened by the war (Grappelli moved to London and Reinhardt stayed in France), Reinhardt's reputation was secure and he was invited to join Duke Ellington's band as a featured soloist for a tour in 1946. He took up the electric guitar during the 1940s, but retained his taste and subtlety with it, and in his later years became interested in composition. His solo style broadened in scope and resources, and though his vagueness about business dealings and timekeeping prevented his later career from progressing as energetically as it might, at its best Reinhardt's music continued to provide some of the most graceful and evocative sounds in jazz. He died unexpectedly in 1953, but left two sons, Lousson and Babik, who both developed careers as jazz guitarists.

Django Reinhardt, the gypsy jazz genius, in the 1930s. Reinhardt was one of the few European jazz musicians of the time whose reputation crossed the Atlantic, and his distinctive octave-playing style was greatly extended by Wes Montgomery.

WES MONTGOMERY

Montgomery blended jazz guitar styles drawn from Benny Goodman's star guitarist Charlie Christian's thrilling solos, gypsy musician Django Reinhardt, and later from bop guitarists Barney Kessel and Jimmy Raney. From Christian, Montgomery borrowed phrasing and harmonic awareness, and a spectacular broadening of the stock of scales and modes available to improvising that was brought about by bebop's use of advanced chord structures. From Reinhardt he adopted and developed a technique based on octaves rather than on single notes, which required acrobatic slides the length of the

Wes Montgomery not only created great jazz, he also appeared to enjoy every moment of it in his prime. He was the most natural and instinctive of improvisers.

youngest was pianist Charles 'Buddy' Montgomery, a pianist of the Bud Powell bebop style who also had a soft spot for Art Tatum.

Wes Montgomery married young and acquired responsibilities fast (he had six children in rapid succession in the early years of his marriage, and a seventh later). Early in his working life in a factory, and to the initial chagrin of his wife, he spent $300, probably two months' wages, on a new guitar, amplifier and box of picks, without bothering to pass through the usual aspiring musician's route of borrowing or buying second-hand instruments before investing in new equipment of his own.

'Montgomery stunned the guitar world and still does, but he also astonished musicians of every kind.'

fingerboard and accurate shaping of the left hand to deaden the unused strings – hard at any tempo, but particularly at bop speeds. Moreover he developed a bop piano-like 'comping' technique, a method of accompaniment and occasional solo embellishment using four-string chords that, in Montgomery's hands, expanded into a full-blown solo style.

But beyond all his technical skill was the extraordinary grip that Montgomery exerted on his audiences. His energy came from a passionate love of musicianship that was often disguised by the relaxation with which he appeared to be playing. Like Coltrane or Jimi Hendrix, Montgomery's instrument was almost an extension of his body. He played every chance he got – during intermissions at gigs, at home, on journeys, everywhere.

John Leslie 'Wes' Montgomery was born in Indianapolis on 6 March 1925, the middle of three brothers, all of whom became successful jazz musicians. The eldest, William Howard 'Monk' Montgomery, was a double-bassist who switched to electric bass guitar in 1951 for a tour with Lionel Hampton, becoming the first jazz musician to specialise in the instrument; the

As soon as he was reasonably proficient, Montgomery went after as many Indianapolis club gigs as he could talk bandleaders into hiring him for, and hung on for the jam sessions afterwards despite having to get up for his day job the next morning. It was as if he was only half alive when the guitar was not in his hands.

Montgomery did not bother with tutor books, but relied on his ears, and on his eldest brother, who was the best-established of the three brothers on the local music scene. In Indianapolis at the time, there was a blind jazz pianist called Errol Grandy, who favoured an ornate Art Tatum-like style and who regularly threw after-hours jam sessions at his house. Wes and Monk Montgomery began visiting the Grandy sessions, and if he was puzzled, Wes would ask the pianist what he was doing. Grandy might name a chord to him, but as Montgomery didn't know how to write it down he would instead locate its component notes on the guitar by ear – and discover in the process that today's chord might be a part of a different chord which he already knew. By this route,

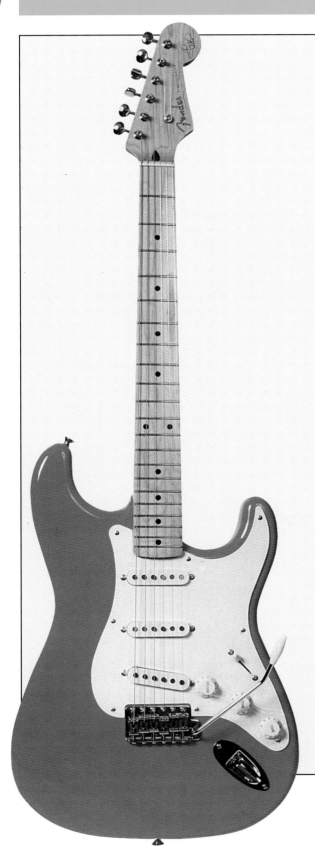

ELECTRIC GUITAR
DESIGN

THE MAJORITY OF GUITARS have six strings and are either hollow-bodied and played without built-in amplification ('acoustic guitars'), or hollow- or solid-bodied guitars fitted with electric pickups ('electric guitars'). In the latter, the vibrations of the strings are converted into electrical signals by a pickup fitted beneath them – sometimes two or more – to detect the variations in tone quality, from metallic and trebly to soft and bassy, obtained when the strings are struck at different distances from the guitar's bridge. The signal transmitted to an amplifer, and converted back into sound waves at the loudspeakers, can also be electronically altered – an extension of the guitarist's vocabulary that has expanded with digital advances in recent years – to produce augmented octaves, overtones, distortion and simulation of other instruments.

The jazz guitar of the 1930s to the 1960s was generally based on a hollow-bodied acoustic design. By the end of the 1920s guitars used in jazz were steel-strung and often arch-topped, like a cello, to increase the instrument's volume. The Gibson L-5, designed by engineer Lloyd Loar and intended for plectrum-playing, was first introduced in 1922 and became the quintessential jazz guitar, with f-holes instead of a circular sound-hole and an adjustable bridge. In 1934 it was expanded in size, and in 1939 it was offered with a cutaway section on the lower half of the sound-box, to facilitate reaching the higher registers.

Gibson's Lloyd Loar began developing magnetic pickups in the 1920s, and around 1935 both Rickenbacker and Gibson produced electric arch-tops. The Fender company produced the first solid-bodied electrics in 1948, and Gibson followed with the 1952 Les Paul. Such instruments are now almost universally used in pop music, and in some jazz ensembles.

Before the widespread use of electric guitars, the other major solo influences of the 1930s were Jimmie Lunceford's Eddie Durham (an early experimenter with amplification), and the dazzling Django Reinhardt. But it was a combination of the virtuosity of Charlie Christian and the celebrity-status of the Benny Goodman Orchestra he played in, that put the electric guitar permanently on the map.

The famous Fender Stratocaster (left). Invented by Leo Fender in the 1950s, it became the archetypal rock guitar, but some jazz musicians have occasionally used it too.

Montgomery learned the relationships between the harmonic structures of chords in his own way, hearing the way they flowed into one another rather than learning individual chords in isolation.

One of the most instantly recognisable features of Montgomery's sound – plucking the strings with his thumb rather that with a pick – came early on. Montgomery told the critic Ralph Gleason:

'. . . in order to get a certain amount of speed you should use a pick, I think. A lot of cats say you don't have to play fast, but being able to play fast can make you phrase better. But I just didn't like the sound. I tried it for about two months. Didn't use the thumb at all. But after two months I still couldn't use the pick, so I said I'd go ahead and use the thumb. But then I couldn't use the thumb either, so I asked myself which are you going to use? I liked the tone better with the thumb, but the technique better with the pick, but I couldn't have them both.'

Montgomery admitted that he never felt comfortable with the pick and constantly dropped it in his early practice sessions. Another virtue of the technique was that it was quieter in a small house: to avoid waking the baby and the neighbours, Montgomery turned his amplifier down low and used his thumb. (Legend also has it that his wife promptly told him how much better he sounded from the moment he adopted the technique.) This new style changed the way he approached Reinhardt's effect of playing in octaves: rather than picking the low and high note of the octave at the same time with the thumb and one finger. Montgomery swept across both with his thumb. In doing this, he trained

himself to stretch his left hand wider in order to play the octave notes on strings that were closer together, as this meant that there were fewer intermediate notes to muffle. The chord technique that he adopted from pianists brought the range and expressiveness of the guitar closer to that of a keyboard while the octaves suggested the sound of a two-horn bebop front line.

Orrin Keepnews, the record producer who was to capture much of Wes Montgomery's finest work for the Riverside label at the beginning of the 1960s, is ambivalent about the virtues of self-tuition, but is sure that the guitarist's unique sound would not have been the same without it:

'The whole question of how much of Wes's impact and strength comes from his being a self-taught musician is tricky. But some of the things that he was most celebrated for are either the things that he shouldn't have done – like he had no business playing guitar that way without using a pick. He had the octave runs, and the block chords, all of the hallmarks of his style are things that if you know enough about music, and you know enough about the guitar, you know can't be done.'

This intuitive approach helped to open up for Montgomery the mysteries of how Charlie Christian's improvised solos were invented: Montgomery learned them note for note, gaining invaluable insights, in the process, into how this music was made on the fly. With his increased technical skill and musical confidence, Montgomery began to be in demand in the Indianapolis clubs. Early on, he adopted the sort of lifestyle that some people suggest may have contributed to his early death from a heart attack, sustaining a variety of manual day jobs to support his growing family and working the

'Wes Montogomery did not bother with tutor books, but relied on his ears.'

nightclubs until the small hours, a combination he sustained until the late 1950s. Orrin Keepnews recalls:

> 'Wes always operated in terms of his responsibility to his family. He had accepted early on the fact that he had the responsibility to his family, but he also had the responsibility to his art, and he spent a lot of time consciously juggling these things and trying to create a life in which he could satisfy both of those needs, to be a responsible husband and father and to be a responsible artist.'

'The way he got around the instrument was simply unheard of before.'

GEORGE BENSON

Out of Charlie Christian's beautifully phrased, cast-from-bronze solos, Montgomery rapidly evolved a sound of his own. His fluency was noticed by Lionel Hampton, a bandleader who was constantly on the watch for upcoming talent (the great jazz singer Betty Carter was one of his early discoveries). From 1948 until 1950, Montgomery toured with the Hampton Orchestra, making brief solo appearances on live radio broadcasts, and recording in a Hampton sub-group with tenor saxophonist Gene Morris and vocalist Sonny Parker.

But family life always drew Montgomery home to Indianapolis, and throughout the early 1950s he remained there. Word sometimes emerged of the guitar virtuoso who sounded like Charlie Christian with Django Reinhardt's harmonic devices thrown in, but the dominance of New York as a jazz centre was unchallenged, except by the new popularity of cooler jazz being made in Los Angeles and San Francisco. Montgomery wouldn't move, and the jazz world wouldn't come to him.

In 1955 Montgomery joined his two brothers and local musicians Alonzo Johnson (saxophone) and Robert Johnson (drums) in the Indianapolis-based Montgomery-Johnson Quintet, the group he was to make some rare early recordings with. But he still kept his day job and, although he was still obsessed with the guitar, his ambitions did not extend to changing the face of jazz (unlike Miles Davis, John Coltrane or Ornette Coleman in other parts of the States). An easy-going, modest man, whose prime concerns were to be a breadwinner for his family and, in his spare time, to play the best bop guitar he could, Wes Montgomery was happy to play with his brothers and his friends and to be a home boy.

He may have continued in this way for the rest of his life had not Monk and Buddy Montgomery branched out. Monk moved to Seattle for a while, and Buddy followed, after which the two travelled on to San Francisco to try their luck on a West-Coast jazz scene that was teeming with life in the 1950s. Buddy was playing vibes as much as piano, and a breezier, less closeted variation on the soft, chiming music of the popular Modern Jazz Quartet appealed to him and Monk.

In 1957, Monk and Buddy formed a group called The Mastersounds on the West Coast which rapidly became a success on the San Francisco scene. Wes Montgomery occasionally joined it, and the group was augmented by other West Coast musicians for a series of unpretentious but infectiously swinging recording sessions.

In later interviews, Wes Montgomery was to observe that he believed he was playing at his best in those years. Compared to recordings he made when the wider jazz world woke up to him at the end of the decade, his sound in this period is a little leaner, sharper and less rounded in tone, but the ease with which he throws off glowingly

CHARLIE CHRISTIAN

CHARLIE CHRISTIAN WAS BORN in Texas on 29 July 1916 and died in New York on 2 March 1942. He was a key member of the coterie of young swing-band musicians who founded the bebop movement, and his methods inspired virtually all the bop guitarists who immediately followed him. Christian was one of the early users of electric amplification for guitar. He worked with a variety of Oklahoma touring bands before the impresario John Hammond introduced him to the bandleader Benny Goodman. Christian started a jazz legend by improvising for a full 90 minutes on a single tune, 'Rose Room', on his audition, and his appearances with Goodman's orchestra made him a celebrity. A sensational 1941 recording of 'Solo Flight' memorably records their relationship.

Yet Christian's most lasting contribution to jazz was made at the venues he attended after hours – notably Minton's Playhouse in Harlem, where other young jazz experimenters such as Charlie Parker, Dizzy Gillespie and Thelonious Monk also went. Like that famous triumvirate, Christian had a sophisticated harmonic imagination: his improvisations were based on complex chords and fast-moving combinations of chords, and their related scales. Christian's improvisations were thus reminiscent of a saxophone player at work, rather than any previous guitar improviser. Charlie Christian's remarkable career was cut short by tuberculosis, but countless guitarists, including Wes Montgomery, followed him.

Charlie Christian in the late 1930s. Note the single electric pickup under the strings. Christian didn't invent the electric guitar, but he had the boldest, most harmonically sophisticated and original style on it of anyone before Wes Montgomery, and he was the original architect of bebop too.

Wes Montgomery used a succession of standard Gibson L5 guitars, but modified the pickups to restore an edge to the sound muffled by his thumbing technique – and had inlays set in the top where his fingers rested to prevent the woodwork from being chafed away.

vibrant and gracefully shaped improvisations is already obvious. The sound of this Montgomery band was a throwback to a cool-jazz group that the guitarist had admired six years previously – the pairing of the tersely romantic tenor saxophonist Stan Getz with guitarist Jimmy Raney from 1951, a period that was possibly the most fertile and inventive of Getz's career.

In April 1958, Wes and Montgomery recorded with a superb West Coast tenor saxophonist, Harold Land – a Texan raised in California, with a dry, almost melancholy sound and striking purity of tone, who had worked in Max Roach and Clifford Brown's famous hard bop quintet. The Montgomery–Land session reveals the guitarist's influences more explicitly than later recordings – notably the sinewy, business-like qualities of both Raney and Tal Farlow, who were among Montgomery's favourite guitar players after Charlie Christian.

Wes Montgomery's recordings from this period still don't sound like a man trying to impose his stamp on his surroundings. He was 34, but although his improviser's talents were largely honed by now and he was frequently the most striking soloist on these sessions, he appeared to have few ambitions for leadership. But Monk and Buddy were no longer on the doorstep, and in 1959 Wes

THE GUITAR
& THE ORGAN

THE HAMMOND ORGAN was introduced in 1935, and its portability made it attractive to jazz musicians on the road. Advances in its construction meant that by 1950 it was an instrument of considerable versatility, with a cutting and percussive sound, wild and turbulent tremolo (the product of its unique rotating Leslie speaker system) and a capacity for thrilling climactic effects. Associations with its predecessor, the pipe organ, made the Hammond popular in gospel and soul music as well as in jazz, with the result that when a form of bebop strongly flavoured by blues, gospel and soul – hard bop – became popular in the mid-1950s, the instrument came into its own.

These associations with more raw and fundamental roots of jazz involved the Hammond in a number of productive relationships with instruments equally effective in a rootsier style – particularly the tenor saxophone and the guitar. Although the organ had been creatively explored in pre-war jazz by Fats Waller, Glenn Hardman and Count Basie, it was Jimmy Smith in the mid-1950s who revolutionised the Hammond by playing up-tempo bebop lines on it, and combining them with a churning, raunchy chordal sound drawn from gospel and church music that effectively balanced funkiness and melodic intricacy.

Smith made the double bass all but irrelevant in organ bands by perfecting a pedalling technique that effectively replicated the 'walk' of a bebop bass player. He thus became a rhythm section on his own, and organ-based groups grew in popularity not only because the sound suited the hard-bop and soul-jazz fashion of the late 1950s, but also because it allowed promoters to hire fewer musicians. Both Smith (with long-time guitar associate Kenny Burrell) and Wes Montgomery liked the guitar-organ combination, and the latter's extensive use of the blues fitted well with the disposition of most organists. The Indianapolis band

Montgomery led shortly before his discovery by Cannonball Adderley and Riverside Records featured a reserved but imaginatively supportive local organist, Mel Rhyne, who performed on some of the early Riverside sessions. But Montgomery's most famous organ collaborations were with Jimmy Smith himself, on the 'Dynamic Duo' recordings for Verve in 1966.

Among contemporary guitarists, John McLaughlin has often favoured partnership with organists influenced by the Smith approach – notably the late Larry Young (who introduced modal and free-jazz techniques to the Hammond) in the 1970s, and with Joey DeFrancesco in the 1990s.

Organist Jimmy Smith, 'The Cat'. Smith married the hot gospel sound of the Hammond organ to a bebop pianist's dexterity and complexity, and the blues and funky qualities of his music were usually complemented by the presence of guitarists. Smith and Wes Montgomery had several musical meetings.

THE JAZZ GUITAR
& POP HEROES

Until the 1960s, jazz and rock guitarists remained worlds apart. Although blues guitar stars like T-Bone Walker appeared on jazz packages such as Norman Granz's *Jazz at the Philharmonic* shows, before the 1960s the guitar was used primarily as a rhythm instrument in rock and pop, with solos rarely lasting longer than a chorus.

But during the 1960s and early 1970s bands like *The Grateful Dead* featured spontaneous playing based on modal principles, like their contemporaries in jazz, as well as contributions from virtuoso guitarist Jerry Garcia. British guitarist Eric Clapton, in a variety of blues bands and then in the power trio *Cream* (partnered by former jazz musicians, bassist

Jack Bruce and drummer Ginger Baker) showed how eloquent and spontaneous a rock guitarist could be. But perhaps the most influential of these guitarists was Jimi Hendrix.

Hendrix, an American blues and rock guitarist who moved to England during the 1960s, astonished musicians of all kinds. Not only did he exhibit great fluency and suppleness of line, and an ability to improvise compellingly at length, he seemed to reflect some of the tonal departures of 1960s free-form jazz in his howling, wailing sound (assisted by fuzz and wah-wah electronics) and indifference to conventional harmonic and scale-playing rules. Hendrix influenced many younger jazz guitarists, even postboppers like the popular John Scofield, but his boldness also touched other instrumentalists – Miles Davis, putting his trumpet through a wah-wah in the 1970s, sounds distinctly like a minimalist Jimi Hendrix.

Today many musicians are influenced by Wes Montgomery's graceful approach – audible in the work of jazz guitarists who bridged the worlds of jazz, rock and soul like George Benson and Lee Ritenour, or those who developed jazzy but highly accessible forms of fusion, like the lyrical Pat Metheny.

Some jazz virtuosi have attempted to make the electric guitar more self-sufficient, as Stanley Jordan has done with his 'tapping' technique in his fretting hand, creating the effect of a simultaneous bassline and boppish single line solo. The legacy of Django Reinhardt, the 1960s, British rhythm & blues scene, and then Miles Davis, jazz-rock fusion, and Indian classical music, come together in the explosive vitality of British expatriate John McLaughlin. New York musician David Gilmour fuses more metallic, rock-derived tonality with postbop melodic complexity. And connections between jazz-guitar lineage and contemporary black pop and soul are made by Britons Ronny Jordan, who had a pop hit with a remake of Miles Davis classic 'So What', and Tony Remy, a brilliant soul-jazz rhythm player with a pungent, unerstated solo style.

For most listeners, the sound of an electric guitar has been defined by its use in pop and rock hard-edged and distorted, sustained and wailing, or backing a band with choppy chords. But Briton Tony Remy (above) is one of many fine soul and funk players who understand the jazz impulse.

Wes (right) was obsessed with the guitar, and treated it as an extension of himself. Like a pool player supporting a cue, his fingers make a bridge on the guitar body, supporting the all-important thumb.

Montgomery did take the plunge – forming a guitar-organ trio with local keyboardist Mel Rhyne and a variety of drummers. The band was heard on its home patch by the celebrated alto saxophonist Julian 'Cannonball' Adderley, who immediately returned to New York to burst into the office of Riverside Records boss Orrin Keepnews, proclaiming: 'There's this guitarist in Indianapolis, and we've got to get him for the label.' Orrin Keepnews takes up the story:

'Cannonball was very, very persuasive and forceful. I was so convinced that within a matter of days I flew out to Indianapolis, spent an evening listening to Wes at his regular evening job. After a slight pause he went on to his after-hours club. He finished work at six in the morning, and I'd been listening to him since about nine o'clock the night before. In a very melodramatic fashion as dawn broke over Indianapolis, over the American Mid-West, I whipped a contract form out of my pocket, and he signed.

'As I later came to understand it, the hard work had been done, Cannonball had told him about this record company that he was with, and said I'm gonna do what I can to get them interested in you. So the shoe was sort of on the other foot, he was kind of waiting for us to come, but I still treasure the positive melodrama of that moment.'

That moment led to a series of superb Montgomery albums for Riverside, frequently with premier-league rhythm sections and front-line partners. At last, Wes Montgomery was about to receive the national recognition that he had deserved for over a decade.

The Incredible Jazz Guitar of Wes Montgomery, an early Riverside date that is now widely regarded as one of his most expressive and technically astonishing recordings, featured the pianist Tommy Flanagan, a musician of considerable empathy and restrained virtuosity who was to be one of Ella Fitzgerald's favourite keyboard partners. Flanagan remembers that Wes Montgomery's reputation had preceded him:

'His legend arrived before he did. You know, "There's this wonderful guitarist in Indianapolis and he's coming to New York". I just happened to be one of the lucky ones that was on one of his first dates. He was truly an exceptional guitarist. He knew the standard songs, but he didn't play them in the standard way. I was the only other soloist and Wes played his opening single-string, and then he'd play the start of the middle chorus, and he was solo playing in octaves. After he had finished that chorus, I was ready to come in, but he started another solo that was in chords, so

6 WES
MONTGOMERY

At times, Wes Montgomery sounded as if he was trying to combine the impact of all the musicians in a band. His fast, smooth, melody-in-chords technique is in use here, mimicking the effect of a pianist.

he played a couple of choruses playing all in chords. It was probably not unheard of to people who had heard Wes before, but to us it was unheard of.

'He was just a natural, you know. It just seemed like nothing he played could be wrong. That's the way he heard it, and that's the way it came out, he just heard things in his head perfectly and they came out that way. Errol Garner was like that too.'

But if Wes Montgomery's improvised music seemed to others to emerge perfectly formed from his consciousness, it never seemed like that to him. He was constantly striving to improve his own sound, both through work on his technique and on his equipment. Orrin Keepnews also recalls the perfectionist side of Montgomery's nature, one that could sometimes be a source of bafflement or exasperation to others. The producer admits he sometimes felt like that himself:

'Wes Montgomery was an incredible, aggravating perfectionist. In my experience with him, he probably never felt that he had performed satisfactorily on any recording. My experience with him is full of takes which I thought were just absolutely fine, which everybody else in the room thought was fine, and Wes said, "Can we do one more, you know, I didn't like my solo". It's amazing how many times the notation on a take from my recordings sessions with Wes would be "WM doesn't like his solo". And once, "WM doesn't like his solo, but everybody else does".'

As he began to work in more challenging and unfamiliar situations than those of his hometown's night life, Montgomery felt inhibited by his lack of formal musical training and his difficulty in reading scores. But although performing with classical musicians on more ambitious recording sessions made him nervous at first, he had grown used to the idea on one of his last recordings with Keepnews at Riverside. Tommy Flanagan remembers:

'I heard that Wes was really shocked when he went to one date to work with an arranger, Jimmy Jones, and he had a string section for him. It made him so nervous, you know, "all these people". He was thinking, "I can't really, you know, I don't read music, and look at all those strings and all this business". Until he heard the first playbacks. He was just perfect, and he was astounded. I think that really eased things for him.'

In 1960 Montgomery briefly moved to San Francisco to rejoin his brothers, a period in which he also made some unrecorded appearances with John Coltrane. The following year he returned to Indianapolis, working once again with his trio – and excellent Riverside albums continued to emerge, many featuring soloists of comparable inventiveness and fluency such as saxophonist Johnny Griffin, and Miles Davis' pianist Wynton Kelly. But Riverside Records was too much of a buff's label to adapt to a musical world in which rock 'n' roll was growing increasingly sophisticated and complex. Riverside hit financial trouble, and in 1964 Montgomery signed with Verve Records, the label founded by jazz impresario Norman Granz. Although Granz was an energetic jazz lover and a celebrated political liberal who

'Wes Montgomery was the quintessential jazz guitarist to me, the quintessential guitar player.' ADRIAN INGRAM, AUTHOR

had done much to awaken the wider American public to the achievements of its African-American population, Verve was a far more conservative and market-oriented organisation than Riverside. Its principal producer in the 1960s was Creed Taylor, a shrewd judge of those elements of a jazz musician's sound that might be massaged for a mass audience. Taylor believed that Montgomery's soft tone and thick, lustrous chords, rather than his flying runs and daring phrasing would find a new kind of fan. It was a watershed in Wes Montgomery's career as significant as Cannonball Adderley's ecstatic endorsement only five years before.

In 1964, working with Taylor, Montgomery began a series of albums with big bands. The long, single-line runs were cut back and the silky octave passages and mellow, swinging chord passages were made more prominent. The financial success that he felt had eluded him (Keepnews had consoled him back in those days saying, 'Until now you were a bum and broke; now you're a star and broke. That's real progress.') now came quickly. Montgomery's chordal exposition of the pop song 'Goin' Out of My Head' (1965) won a Grammy award, and most of his Verve output did very well by the usual standards of jazz instrumental sales. Many of Montgomery's earlier fans felt that his greatest strengths had been silenced by this process. However Blue Note producer Michael Cuscuna, an informed judge of both jazz performances and of the pressures on a record company, takes neither Montgomery or Verve to task.

'What Creed Taylor was doing with Wes Montgomery was essentially making pop records. But at the same time a lot of people forget that he was recording Wes Montgomery at the Half Note with the Wynton Kelly Trio too. So you know, Wes did have two sides to his recording aspect, and Creed Taylor was always very successful doing crossover records. It never ever hurt jazz to have Stan Getz on top ten radio, or 'California Dreaming' by Wes Montgomery or 'Mercy, Mercy, Mercy' by Cannonball Adderley. That can only heighten the awareness of jazz and possibly draw

MONTGOMERY'S
TECHNIQUES

IN EARLY JAZZ, the guitar inherited the banjo's role as a rhythm instrument only, and the louder arch-top was invented to make it more prominent in bigger jazz ensembles. The move to guitar was also encouraged by the popularity of Paul Whiteman's guitarist Eddie Lang, a brilliant technician. Hero of the strictly rhythm players was Count Basie's Freddie Green, an accompanist of unflappable stability. But there were still relatively few jazz guitar heroes the young Wes Montgomery could turn to for guidance.

Wes Montgomery never learned the guitar as many musicians did. He never had formal lessons, he could not read music, and he didn't even use the standard tuition books that were available for the instrument in the 1940s.

Instead, Montgomery used his ears and the assistance of his brothers and musicians on the Indianapolis jazz scene. The first major departure he made from conventional jazz-guitar melodic technique was to avoid the use of a plectrum, or pick – partly because he disliked the feel and sound of it, and partly because his wife, family and neighbours preferred the quieter sound he obtained plucking with his thumb when practising at home. Montgomery found that the choice imposed both restraints and opportunities for a distinctive style such as his. He couldn't play as fast with the thumb, because a plectrum player can sound notes both on the downstroke and the upstroke – impossible even for the virtuosic Montgomery. Yet the method's reward was a tone of mellow delicacy, richer and more resonant than the twangier sound produced with the plectrum.

A self-taught player with no knowledge of musical theory, Montgomery also developed an insight into harmony from an intuitive understanding of how chords are related. When fellow musicians demonstrated the structure of a particular chord to him, he would hear its inner voicings and their relationship to other chords he knew. He thus evolved a remarkable sense of how progressions of chords could flow, and used this understanding as a solo style in its own right, imparting to his music its characteristic bounce and forward momentum. He also took on an effect that Django Reinhardt, an early favourite, used only sparingly – playing melodies in octaves, two notes spaced by an eight-note interval, one sounding at twice or half the vibrating frequency of the other. They sound the same, yet not the same, and suggest the warm, harmonious feel that Montgomery liked.

Striking across the two notes of the octave with his thumb, rather than finger-picking with the thumb and finger, presented another technical problem if Montgomery was to use Reinhardt's special effect more extensively and at bebop's headlong speeds. Where Reinhardt might have sounded his octave on a fourth-string and a first-string note together, damping or deadening the 'irrelevant' strings between with the inner part of his fingers, Montgomery found that it was difficult to deaden two strings consistently when playing fast with his left hand constantly changing position. He reduced the number of intervening strings from two to one by stretching his left hand in order to finger the same octave notes on strings three and one, instead. This was more of a left-hand contortion, but for his purposes produced a better sound. The Scottish guitarist Jim Mullen says:

> 'When I play octaves, I'm carefully trying to aim for the two notes that I'm trying to play, but Wes could dampen off the notes he didn't want to hear, at real breakneck tempo. That's like defying gravity, almost.'

Wes Montgomery played the Gibson L5, using heavy-gauge, flat-wound strings – the latter preferred to the more traditional wire-wound type, which would have squeaked on his favourite octave-sliding technique. From 1957 he adopted the L-5CES, eventually modified by the Gibson factory to dispense with the treble or bridge pickup, although he balanced this brassier sound against the cutting power delivered by using a metal rather than a wooden bridge. Montgomery had an inlay in the shape of a heart installed on the lower body of one of his guitars, and the shape of a diamond with his name placed underneath on another. It was a decoration, but it had a practical and very necessary purpose. Montgomery's unique plucking technique, with his thumb swinging free and his fingers propped on the body for support, had led to his fingernails wearing a hole through the woodwork of his first instruments.

Scottish guitarist Jim Mullen is one of the few musicians to use Wes' thumb-picking technique – although there is a stronger blues and rhythm-and-blues flavour to his playing. Mullen describes the speed of Montgomery's inimitable octave runs as 'like defying gravity'.

more people into it. Whether you like it or not, a lot of commercial records should not be castigated, because they get jazz further into other people's faces than any pure jazz could ever go.'

Pianist Tommy Flanagan also disputes the widespread belief among the more unforgiving of Montgomery fans that this was the end of the guitarist's creative life.

'I don't think it was a trap. If it was, it was a good one. It was his style, and it was great, it's been used all over, now everybody does it. I don't think he ever lost his musical integrity, 'cause his heart was always there.'

'He was just a natural, you know. It seemed like nothing he played could be wrong.' TOMMY FLANAGAN

Certainly Montgomery continued to play superbly in live performance with the fast-moving boppish small-groups that suited him best – sometimes with the Miles Davis pianist Wynton Kelly, sometimes with his brothers. He delivered with his usual infectious enthusiasm and relaxation at Ronnie Scott's Club in Britain in 1965, and the downsizing of his skills in the Verve studios seemed to have left no lasting impact on his massive capabilities.

Orrin Keepnews, who saw Wes Montgomery close to his best in the recording studio, does not agree, however. Although he acknowledges that his judgement may be biased, Keepnews feels that what happened later was the result of inappropriate guidance for a man who hated having to take all-or-nothing decisions for himself, but who also hated doing less than his best.

'Going to Verve was as much Riverside leaving him as him leaving Riverside, because Wes was one of the artists who was with the label until it ran into its huge financial difficulties and foundered and died in 1964. But when Wes went on to work with Creed Taylor at Verve and at A&M, what happened was he got caught up in the process. Irrationally perhaps, I still feel that his quite early death was, in part, due to the tremendous emotional strain that I know he was under as a result of recording, and that he himself did not feel comfortable with it. He did not feel he was being true to his art. I know this from talking with him about it.

'. . . Wes was a perfectionist who was never entirely comfortable with his own work, yet not an aggressive man, not an argumentative man. He was one of the most warm, open, delightful human beings it's ever been my pleasure to know. One of a handful of musicians that I like to feel my relationship with them could have existed even if music hadn't been involved in the equation at all. But I've always felt if he had asserted himself, if he had said to the people in his new recording circumstances, "Look, I'm making a lot of money for you, and I'm not that happy with what I'm doing, I'll make a deal with you, I'll do two albums for you and the third one will be for me". . . but the man who could have said that would not have been the real Wes Montgomery.'

In 1968, Wes Montgomery shocked the jazz world by dying suddenly in Indianapolis, from a heart attack. Guitarist Adrian Ingram, a Montgomery discographer and biographer who has made a closer study of the musician's contribution than most, assesses his impact:

'Wes Montgomery was the quintessential jazz guitarist to me, the quintessential guitar player. When I stumbled across a Wes Montgomery recording, it totally floored me – and although I would have been 14 at the time, I decided that what I wanted to do for

'I don't think he
ever lost his
musical integrity,
'cause his heart
was always there.'

TOMMY FLANAGAN

If Wes Montgomery had not died
of a heart attack in his early 40s,
he would have seen how
profoundly his improvising genius
influenced younger guitarists –
rather than the easy-listening
music that made him a big star.

the rest of my life was to play the guitar. I still get that feeling every time I listen to Wes's wonderful, timeless playing. Wes obviously wouldn't be as well known, or perhaps as influential, as people like Eric Clapton, Keith Richards and George Harrison. But even the rock players and blues players liked what he did. Most every guitar player that you'll speak to will have a soft spot for Wes Montgomery, and say how influential he's been.'

The last word belongs to George Benson, the musician whose personal development of the Montgomery style has helped make him one of the best-known guitarists in the world. When future generations assess the first century of jazz, Benson says:

'They're going to have to mention the Montgomerys and the Charlie Parkers and the John Coltranes because there is nobody who's made a greater impression in the music world. They are innovators of the first kind, when they touch their instruments they affect the whole world, you know, it's a slow fire that burns right through the industry and it affects everybody. It elevates the music from where it was, and it takes it to another place.'

7 CHAPTER

JOHN
COLTRANE

'In his music there's a great
spirituality, a great kindness,
a generosity, a focus and
a dedication, sometimes
bordering on obsession.
And there's humility.'

JOSHUA REDMAN, SAXOPHONIST

WHEN JOHN COLTRANE, one of the most temperamentally gentle performers ever to release a musical firestorm, died of liver cancer at 40 in 1967, the event hit much of the jazz world as if a celestial catastrophe had suddenly put out the sun.

Coltranes' death affected the jazz musicians of the time in different ways. Some like the saxophonist Anthony Braxton, decided on radical changes to their music, as a mark of respect and of acceptance that a unique artist's departure demanded that they now fend for themselves. A few gave up playing altogether. Musicians and listeners everywhere, in jazz and outside it, started counting the ways in which Coltrane had changed their lives, much as had happened after the premature death of the previous jazz messiah, Charlie Parker, two decades before. Some, like the gifted pianist Keith Jarrett, considered that Coltrane would have been typically forward thinking in his response: 'He didn't intend to leave a gap – he intended that there be more space for everybody to do what they should do'.

The ripples from Coltrane's brilliant career continued to be felt. Contemporary composers including Phillip Glass, LaMonte Young and Terry Riley, none of them jazz musicians, have acknowledged debts to Coltrane's turbulent genius. The Coltrane legacy surfaces everywhere, from 1960s rock celebrities like the Byrds, (whose 'Eight Miles High' is a Coltrane homage), the Allman Brothers and Carlos Santana to pop-jazz star Kenny G (probably the best-known saxophonist in the world today). Young British sax virtuoso Courtney Pine's 1990s' popular blend of funk, free-jazz and hip-hop is rooted in Coltrane's sound and technique. And young American saxophonist Joshua Redman, one of the most accomplished improvisers in the contemporary jazz world, acknowledges the extent of Coltrane's influence:

'John Coltrane is one of the most influential musicians ever. The passion of his music is timeless, the spirituality of his music is timeless, the emotional depth of the music is timeless – not to mention his technique as a saxophonist and his innovations in terms of harmony, melody and all the technical elements. In his music there's a great spirituality, a great kindness, a generosity, a focus and a dedication, sometimes bordering on obsession. And there's humility.'

In his prime, Coltrane seemed to pack a lifetime of artistic evolution into just a few years. He often discussed music as if advancing it were his mission. A strong constitution, undermined early on by drugs and alcohol, may have compounded this mission with a sense that he was working on borrowed time. Coltrane's achievements seemed to fall over each other to make their impact on the world of jazz. As if stretching jazz materials one way and then another to find their breaking point, Coltrane first took the bebop fundamentals of chord progressions and redoubled even the complexity they had acquired at Charlie Parker's hands – and then having developed a hurtling jazz vehicle in which a chord might change on every beat, he scrapped it all for a music based on scales, with hardly any chordal movement at all.

In the 1960s Coltrane became famous for brilliant quartet music of rumbling, distinctly Africanised, rhythmic momentum, but after four years he turned that into a music in which the 'beat' seemed to have vanished, or to have been supplanted by a feel as primal and diffuse as the impact of waves on rocks. He developed breathing and fingering techniques that created the illusion of more than one saxophone playing at the same time. He also rescued the little-used soprano saxophone from obscurity and gave it a dominant voice – the principal reason why Kenny G, a musician at the other end of the scale to Coltrane in intensity and imaginative boldness, plays it now. Coltrane was also a pioneer of 'world music' and of the expansion of audiences' aural consciousness to a widespread acceptance of non-western notions of tone purity and pitch.

John Coltrane frequently delivered marathon performances, in which a saxophone improvisation on a single theme might run for an hour or more. He informed his one-time boss Miles Davis that once he got started he didn't know how to stop playing, occasioning Davis' famous riposte, 'Try taking the saxophone out of your mouth'. In response to a similar enquiry from Davis on another occasion, Coltrane merely said, 'It took that long to get it all in'. However, it is clear that on many occasions he entered a trance-like state when he was playing and was simply unaware of how much time had actually passed.

Although the furious pace at which Coltrane's mature music evolved had the effect of burning off layers of his audience as he explored each stage and moved on, his relative popularity in the 1960s was in part due to his gift for reaching out to ordinary listeners. He emotionally involved the audience, often at first hearing, in musical departures that were technically complex, and which in other hands would have had them running for the exits.

John Coltrane, later known simply as 'Trane' was born on 23 September 1926 in Hamlet, North Carolina, and raised with his cousin Mary by John Robert and Alice Blair Coltrane. His father was a tailor who also played the violin and clarinet, and his mother had studied music, and sang and played the piano in the Baptist church of her preacher father – an influence from religious music that deepened when the family went to live with Alice's parents in High Point, North Carolina, when John was three. But when John's father, grandfather, and uncle all died in the same year, 1939, Alice travelled north for work to Atlantic City, New Jersey.

John Coltrane took up the alto horn, clarinet, and then alto saxophone, playing both in the orchestra at William Penn High School, and beginning to make heroes of such famous sax players of the day as tenorist Lester Young and Duke Ellington's breathy, romantic altoist, Johnny Hodges. In 1943, John Coltrane graduated, moved from Atlantic City to Philadelphia to work in a sugar refinery, and studied alto saxophone formally at the Ornstein School of Music and the Granoff Studios. Alice and Mary followed him to Philadelphia in 1944, and the following year John, now 19, began playing professionally, and performed on clarinet with a navy band in 1945.

'John Coltrane is one of the most influential musicians ever.'

JOSHUA REDMAN, SAXOPHONIST

THE TENOR SAX

Coltrane at full throttle in the '60s, eyes closed, in a musical trance that could last hours. Coltrane extended the range of the tenor saxophone in ways never previously thought possible – into a soprano-like upper register, into simultaneous notes resembling chords, and into warp-speed improvisations.

ORNETTE COLEMAN ONCE claimed that the most powerful musical revelations by black Americans 'of what their soul is' had been made on the tenor saxophone. From the early 1930s onwards, this flexible, articulate horn, spanning reverberating church-organ low notes to a pure, piccolo falsetto, rivalled the trumpet as the dominant jazz instrument. The basis of the range covered by the tenor saxophone is from low A flat to E flat two octaves above middle C, but since the innovations of John Coltrane, many saxophonists play much higher than that. There is a single reed, set in a mouthpiece that may be hard rubber, ebonite, plastic or metal – John Coltrane preferred the latter. There is a key high on the tube, close to the neck, that shifts the register from one octave to another, but although the springing and action of the pads has been improved during the jazz era, the tenor sax is still largely as it was when Coleman Hawkins brought it to life.

Until the late 1920s, there were few strong improvisers among saxophonists – Sidney Bechet, adapting a clarinet style to the soprano sax, was the most prominent, but his technique was a transplanted one, not developed specifically for the instrument. Bechet's protégée, Johnny Hodges, came next on alto. Coleman Hawkins was influenced by improvising performers that history has forgotten, such as Prince Robinson and Stump Evans, but Hawkins, with his big sound, irresistable momentum, whirring vibrato and harmonic insights, was truly the originator of the tenor saxophone as a jazz voice.

Although he originally played the clarinet, Hawkins used the tenor saxophone almost exclusively from 1924, and rapidly developed a flowing style from the staccato 'slap-tonguing' technique that was usually employed for the instrument. Hawkins also understood musical theory, and as his playing evolved, the chord-based improvising of pianist Art Tatum influenced him as much as any reed technique.

Coleman Hawkins, the father of the tenor saxophone in jazz. Hawkins rescued it from dance-band and vaudeville obscurity, and created a vocabulary to which most subsequent tenorists referred. Miles Davis is on the right.

By the end of the 1920s, Hawkins was influencing nearly all upcoming tenorists, including Chu Berry, Herschel Evans and Ben Webster, who later became swing-band celebrities, and later soloists like Illinois Jacquet Flip Phillips, Buddy Tate and Don Byas, and eventually tenor genius Sonny Rollins.

Lester Young was as significant an influence on the tenor saxophone as Hawkins, but he had a totally contrasting style. Unusually for a black instrumentalist, Young was influenced by the lighter, gentler sound of white saxophonists Frankie Trumbauer (who was associated with Paul Whiteman) and Jimmy Dorsey. Unlike Hawkins, the underlying chords of a song were of less interest to Young — and although he intuitively grasped harmonic movement, he preferred to manipulate the melody line, with constant detailed variation of texture and accent in the manner of Louis Armstrong, but from a more oblique angle. Young played down the effect of vibrato, and varied it from an occasional Hawkins-like throb to a barely perceptible quiver. His influence on the original bop movement

and the 'cool school' that followed it was immense. Charlie Parker's early solos sounded like Young solos speeded up and post 1940s players including Stan Getz, Lee Konitz, Zoot Sims and Warne Marsh studied him closely, and his influence even spread to Dexter Gordon, Sonny Rollins and John Coltrane.

Hawkins, Young and Parker, with a little help from Monk, shaped the next great tenor star, Sonny Rollins. Rollins develops solos as quirkily and lyrically as Young, but adds bursts of Parkeresque speed and Hawkins' booming sound. Rollins' influence can be heard in the playing of Joe Henderson today.

Probably the most famous tenor saxophonist in jazz history was John Coltrane. Coltrane's disciples are too numerous to list, but some of the best known are Michael Brecker, George Coleman, Bob Berg and the brilliant Wayne Shorter. In the free-jazz movement of the 1960s, the short-lived Albert Ayler used some of Coltrane's techniques in an even more abstract manner. He actually managed to manipulate made the tenor sax to produce a sound that resembled a human cry.

In the late 1940s in Philadelphia, Coltrane took a familiar path for a black saxophonist in an industrial town at that time. He played rhythm 'n' blues, taking up the gutsier tenor sax to play with the earthy Texan saxophonist and blues singer Eddie 'Cleanhead' Vinson in 1948. He also played for a while in the bands of the Tulsa saxophonist Earl Bostic. Bostic was a soloist of idiosyncratic mannerisms, favouring glissandos and vibrato laid on heavily – but he also had a knack for making hit records in a bluesy bop manner. Bostic's wailing alto-sax technique, using harmonics in the instrument's upper register that were rarely deployed by the saxophonists of the time, appealed to the young Coltrane. So, crucially for his artistic momentum and physical health,

John Coltrane may have dominated the avant-garde, but his roots were in both bebop and the blues. His early jobs in blues-town Philadelphia were in rhythm-and-blues bands.

did narcotics and alcohol – sirens of the bop subculture whose high priest was legendary jazz genius and gargantuan user Charlie Parker.

In 1949 both Coltrane and fellow Philadelphian and early employer, bandleading saxophonist Jimmy Heath, joined Dizzy Gillespie's celebrated bebop big band. When Gillespie wound the band up under financial pressure in 1950, Coltrane stayed on to play alto in the

RHYTHM
& BLUES

JAZZ WAS CLOSELY ASSOCIATED with blues from the start. The blues was originally a form developed in the southlands in the 19th century by guitarists and singers who blended Arican vocal intonation with European harmonies. Its symmetrical 12-bar form spread quickly among other instrumentalists, saloon pianists developed a driving form of it based on a rocking bass figure and called it boogie-woogie, and blues became a staple form for early jazz bands. In the 1920s, catering for the 'race records' market of black buyers, great blues singers like Bessie Smith and Marnie Smith frequently played with their jazz equivalents, including Louis Armstrong and Coleman Hawkins.

In the Swing era, blues turned into rhythm and blues, a style that not only affected a good deal of 1950s and 1960s jazz, but also rock 'n' roll from Elvis Presley to the Beatles and the Rolling Stones. Saxophonist and singer Louis Jordan's Tympany Five was a very popular early example. Jordan had sung for Chick Webb, and 1949's *Saturday Night Fish Fry* was an epochal hit. The label for this music was 'Jump', a reference to the high-energy dancing that went back to late 1930s hit swing titles like Count Basie's 'One O'Clock Jump'. The Tympany Five used a typical small-band jazz lineup and emphasised swing's repeated riffing technique. Another leading exponent of jump and early rhythm and blues was the Houston saxophonist and singer Eddie 'Cleanhead' Vinson, who had worked in the South with blues guitarist and singer Big Bill Broonzy in the eatly 1940s, with Duke Ellington's trumpeter Cootie Williams later in that decade, and then in a band of his own that included John Coltrane.

New Orleans came back into blues prominence through Fats Domino, a boogie pianist with an affecting voice, and the Los Angeles guitarist and singer T-Bone Walker. Pee Wee Crayton, a West Coast bandleader and an exciting guitarist employed saxophonist Ornette Coleman. Although Coleman became an inspritational force in the avant-garde and in free-improvised music, his powerful swing and emotional sound were steeped in the blues, and still are.

A king of rhythm-and-blues saxophone, Eddie 'Cleanhead' Vinson. Vinson was a bebopper, but there was an anguished cry to his sound, and his jazz-blues bands were very successful.

trumpeter's new sextet. From the early to the middle 1950s, shifting increasingly to the tenor saxophone, Coltrane's approach leaned heavily toward that of Los Angeles tenorist Dexter Gordon. His big sound with its stamina and vocalised cry was a mix of the 'storytelling' method of Lester Young, the gravity and harmonic awareness of pioneering tenor-liberator Coleman Hawkins, and the headlong phrasing of Charlie Parker. He also came to admire Sonny Rollins, who was the most charismatic, technically masterful and influential tenor saxophonist of the mid-1950s. Rollins was drawing on

'. . . on many occasions he entered a trance-like state and was unaware of how much time had actually passed.'

similar materials from Young, Hawkins and Parker, but an affection for the Caribbean music of his parents, and a kind of intuitive bop-narrative were also influential in assembling his phrasing.

This intuition enabled Rollins to sidestep a central plank of bop-sax technique, the memorising of many alternative 'formulae' of phrase-fragments that could be shuffled and juggled to fit the chord progressions of a wide range of tunes. This technique was brilliantly used by Charlie Parker, but was potentially an enemy of the personal voice. In the early years of Coltrane's career he deployed these formulae rather routinely compared to Parker, particularly at fast tempos. Coltrane's strength was his sound – steely and biting on up-tempo tunes (the result of his preference for a metal mouthpiece), opulent yet haunting on ballads.

Coltrane expressed a fondness for the tremulous sound of Stan Getz, but was primarily devoted to the romantic quiver of Duke Ellington's alto saxophonist Johnny Hodges, an inspiration that deepened during his year with Hodges' own septet, between 1953 and 1954. However the relationship was overshadowed by

Coltrane's continuing struggle with drugs, even though he had become a Muslim in his search for guidance and strength. He found some of this guidance and strength from Naima Grubbs, his wife-to-be, to whom he devoted one of his most moving ballads, simply called 'Naima'.

Between 1955 (the year he married Naima) and 1957, Coltrane took the three other giant strides that dramatically shaped this period of his life, the first of which was joining Miles Davis.

Davis' career had also been slowed by drug dependency from 1949 to 1953. However, after kicking the narcotics, and with typical contrariness, he turned on his own chamber-jazz guru status following the 'Birth of the Cool' collaborations of 1949, assembled a firebreathing hard-bop group, and in 1955 he made a sensational comeback appearance at the Newport Jazz Festival. His new band included John Coltrane, who became the wailing, loquacious counterbalance to Davis' famous musical reserve and sense of space. Davis told the writer Nat Hentoff in the 1950s:

'Coltrane's really something. He's been working on those arpeggios and playing them 50 different ways, and playing them all at once.'

Coltrane had been obsessively studying and memorising arpeggios, the sequential notes of chords, to provide himself with an exhaustive stock of fast-moving melody lines that would be suitable for almost any harmonic architecture that he was likely to encounter in a bop-based ensemble. He was absorbing so much musical information that at first all of it would flood out at the same time at every opportunity. In an attempt to pack even more sound into the cramped apartment of a regular song-based jazz tune, Coltrane also began experimenting with fingering and breathing techiques that would enable him to sound more than one note simultaneously – a formidable technical problem on a non-chordal instrument.

Coltrane's continuing drug and drink problem led to Davis replacing him with Sonny Rollins in 1957, but the change accompanied the second and third decisive awakenings of this period of Coltrane's life. Claiming a religious revelation at his mother's house that year, the saxophonist suddenly found the spiritual strength to overcome heroin and alcohol at last. And then, crucially, he worked with the unorthodox and intractable piano and compositional individualist Thelonious Monk, who was also rebuilding his career after troubles of his own, ranging from an unjust drugs charge to a recording career on hold. In Monk Coltrane found a kindred spirit in rebellious idiosyncrasy and unbending devotion to musical intuitions, whatever the critical and public opinion of the time.

A legendary engagement at the Five Spot Cafe in Greenwich Village in summer and autumn 1957 came to be regarded by some as a historic meeting of minds and energies, comparable to the arrival of Louis Armstrong in King Oliver's Chicago band 35 years before. As it was beginning to do in the hands of an emerging elite of improvisers elsewhere (like the pianist Cecil Taylor and the Texan former rhythm and blues saxophonist Ornette Coleman), the form and shape of bop stretched and finally broke in Coltrane's hands. Unlike Miles Davis, Monk actively encouraged Coltrane's most protracted solos – and moreover encouraged him to use evermore minimalist underpinnings. Coltrane later told Nat Hentoff:

'It got so I would go as far as possible on one phrase until I ran out of ideas. The harmonies got to be an obsession for me. Sometimes I was making jazz through the wrong end of a magnifying glass.'

John Coltrane on tenor in the 1950s. Narcotics and alcohol had slowed his career, but by the end of the decade his endless researches were revolutionising sax-playing and jazz form.

Coltrane also indicated that Monk, with his enthusiasm for dissonance, pushed him further toward the exploration of chord-sounds on the saxophone.

Hentoff reported that, as word spread of the Five-Spot season, musicians were eventually standing 'two and three deep' at the bar, astonished by what they were hearing. Little of this ground-breaking relationship was recorded, although Orrin Keepnews caught some of it for Riverside, and Coltrane captured a lo-fi version of the partnership on his own tape-recorder, reprocessed and released much later.

John Coltrane was recording relatively conventional hard-bop discs for Prestige by 1957 (although only one, *Traneing In*, with Miles Davis's rhythm section, really stood out – not least for its delectable ballad playing) and a single Blue Note date, *Blue Train*, came the same year. It was one of the saxophonist's favourite discs from his formative period, and in its avalanches of solo-sax notes was a telling precursor of what Coltrane was soon to do to chord-based improvisation.

The writer Ira Gitler coined the phrase 'sheets of sound' to describe the Coltrane's arpeggio-monsoons. But, as fast as he was building this massive and ornate edifice, Coltrane was simultaneously dismantling it, partly under the influence of the more minimalist Miles Davis. Never a whole-hearted fan of frenetic bebop chord-running, Davis was, by the end of the 1950s, ready to drop them in favour of shifting cycles of note-patterns or modes, a principle closer to Indian music.

Coltrane had briefly studied Indian music with master sitar-player Ravi Shankar in the 1950s (Shankar observed how perplexing he had found the contrast between the American's peaceful, generous demeanour and the ferocity of much of his music) and was attracted to the distinctly different tonalities and interval-systems of non-western music. When he appeared on Miles Davis' most famous early-modal session, *Kind of Blue* (1959), Coltrane sounded like a man who was finding his place in the musical world. On such classic tracks as 'So What', and 'All Blues', Coltrane seemed to combine a gospel singer's stately force, with the stark tenderness of

> **'In Monk Coltrane found a kindred spirit in rebellious idiosyncrasy and unbending devotion to musical intuitions, whatever the critical and public opinion of the time.'**

ballad delivery, and a logic, momentum and continuity in denser improvisations that had lost the repetitiveness of the earlier bop-arpeggio style.

As the 1950s closed, Coltrane was still suspended between two worlds. His flat-out, virtuoso performance on his own 'Giant Steps' (made in May, 1959, after a move to Atlantic Records) was breathtaking even by his exacting standards, the constantly changing chords flying by like station-signs viewed from a speeding train. He could now play so fast as to all but camouflage the formula-shuffling melodic approach of late-bebop. But the next year's 'My Favourite Things' revealed a new clarity. It came in a transitional period in which the leader was experimenting with different personnel, trying out the lighter soprano saxophone, and beginning to explore split tones and multiphonic effects to produce ghostly, vapourous sounds. Saxophonist Evan Parker casts some revealing light on the period's fast progress:

> 'Multiphonics is giving the illusion of producing a chord, more than one pitch is audible in the sound. Usually they're produced by breaking the column of air – that means opening holes above holes that are closed, then if you choose the right combinations you can produce the effect of several notes at the same time. There are many fingering possibilities and each fingering pattern has more than one sound, so it's a whole area of playing which is very rich.'

DRUGS

IT HAS ALWAYS BEEN HARD for jazz musicians to get into the mainstream papers for what they have truly achieved. But until recently, if a reporter could ever be guaranteed to treat a jazz story as anything other than a footnote, it would be when drugs or drink were involved. The few high-profile cases involving arrests or hospitalisation of jazz musicians have been covered out of all proportion to the number who never encoutered such problems, or overcame them, and out of all proportion to the towering positive achievements of these players too. In many minds drugs and jazz have been interchangeable, which reveals how little the music has been investigated or understood by any but those closest to it.

Marijuana, although generally perceived for centuries as a folk medicine rather than a leisure pursuit, has been closely associated with jazz music from the beginning – but since it was almost wholly a working-class relaxation until will into the 20th century, and jazz was a street-life rather than a dinner jacket art for decades, the association isn't surprising and has little to do with the nature of the music itself. Opiates too, were generally medicinal and freely available, but their recreational use bacame associated with the marginalised world of gambling and prostitution as the century turned. Through this route they entered the equally marginalised world of the jazz musician.

Cocaine and marijuana were both freely available in Storyville in the early years of the century – and the latter, in particular, was so popular with jazz musicians that even the music's household names did not consider their reputation tarnished through association with it. But heroin took a more destructive role with the advent of bebop. Some observers suggest that the Mafia may have targetted young musicians of the 1940s who had made money in the Swing bands, realising

Hard drugs hit many musicians of the first and second bebop generation hard. Trumpeter Chet Baker (right) became the favourite jazz subject of some photographers as heroin took hold.

that their pressured late-night lifestyle and ready cash might make them particularly susceptible. The intensity of the jazz-jam session and the drive towards constant, on-the-edge creativity, coupled with exhaustion and fear of failiure in a competitive peer group, may also have made the reduction of apprehension and temporary euphoria that opiates offered an attractive proposition at first. The status that Charlie Parker, in particular, enjoyed in the 1940s also meant that many who wanted to sound like him believed that heroin might be the instant solution. It also took on the role of an initiation rite into the private, twilit world of modern jazz. But Parker himself discouraged the habit in others when he could. 'Don't do as I do, do as I say' he told his young trumpet player Red Rodney.

In his book *The Making of Jazz*, historian James Lincoln Collier suggests that 50-75% of the first generation of bebop players had at least tried hard drugs, that a 25-35% were addicts, and perhaps 20% met an early death as a result.

For all the sweeping technical achievement of 'Giant Steps', Coltrane appeared to regard its recording as a symbolic statement or a landmark rather than an addition to his regular repertoire. Evan Parker said:

> 'He didn't seem to want to play those dense chordal things like "Countdown" or "Giant Steps" live. It was almost as though by documenting them, it was like saying, "Well, this is the formal end of how complex chord sequences can be." When you analyse the solo in "Giant Steps", and when you listen to the alternates which were released later, you see that there are many phrases which crop up in every chorus – as though the thing was a learned etude, that he developed for himself as an exercise.'

For his recording of the jazz-waltz 'My Favourite Things', in October 1960, John Coltrane used the soprano saxophone – a higher-pitched, more plaintive, and at times significantly eastern-toned instrument. The soprano had only one high-profile exponent in jazz before, the great New Orleans musician Sidney Bechet, though a former New Orleans revivalist turned free-improviser called Steve Lacy was using it in the 1950s. Evan Parker explains:

> 'Lacy told me that Coltrane asked him, "Is that a saxophone?" And Lacy said "Yes, it's a soprano, it's the same thing that Sidney Bechet used to play." Then Coltrane immediately knew what that was, but had actually never seen one before that point, this must have been around '58, or '59. He then bought one and started to play it.'

'Sometimes I was making jazz through the wrong end of a magnifying glass.'

JOHN COLTRANE

John Coltrane preferred metal mouthpieces, but sometimes adjusted them so obsessively that they became unplayable. They enhanced his piercing, heartfelt sound.

Ed Jones, a technically powerful young British saxophonist also profoundly influenced by John Coltrane, accounts for the significance of the soprano to 'My Favourite Things':

> 'You can play it on tenor, and it'll sound fine. But there's a much more lyrical, plaintive, haunting sound to the soprano, which serves the melody line much better. Coltrane stripped out all the unnecessary parts of it and turned a show tune into a folk tune – something which is very simple and haunting and raw. He stripped them all out and just based the tune on modes, and when the others were playing behind him, they were just playing on two scales. It brought out the beauty of the melody line.'

That simplicity was a big hit with the general public. The name of Coltrane was spreading fast, way beyond the coterie of insiders and fascinated practitioners who had packed the Five Spot three years before for the brief partnership with Thelonious Monk. Gary Giddins takes up the story:

> '"Giant Steps" and "My Favourite Things" are probably the pinnacle of Coltrane's popularity. "Giant Steps" is a true virtuoso work, so you can't question his technique or his understanding of chords, which was probably the equal of Art Tatum's, at least. It was cutting edge jazz but it was not alienating jazz, you didn't have to have a PhD in jazz studies to understand it.
>
> '"My Favourite Things" was the first record by Coltrane's quartet with Elvin Jones on drums – the first recording that defined the sound of that group and popular way beyond expectation,

GREAT
SMALL BANDS

Though orchestras dominated the jazz firmament for much of the 1930s, and have remained a popular draw ever since, the balance between improvised and composed music (as well as the volatile economics of the jazz business) has led to the small band dominating jazz. Smaller groups permit more open structures, less rehearsal, better audibility for several improvised lines, and understated eye contact between musicians that replaces the conductor in formal music.

The tradition of a motivated ensemble, weaving spontaneous relationships out of brief or perfunctory themes, goes back to the earliest days of jazz. The legendary Charles 'Buddy' Bolden's New Orleans band, working before the invention of the phonograph could capture it for posterity, was a raw pioneering version, probably keeping improvising to a minimum. King Oliver's band was another. But the first to achieve classic status, fundamentally altering the way musicians and listeners perceived jazz, was Louis Armstrong's Hot Five.

Hot Five

Louis Armstrong virtually defined 'swing' with some of his early solos with King Oliver, imparting a feeling of motion to the melody line, placing notes before and behind the beat, and dividing quarter-notes unequally – devices that gave the melody an unprecedented elasticity. But the blazing speed of Armstrong's development in the 1920s is represented in the Hot Five recordings. The recordings began in Chicago in November 1925, with Armstrong on cornet, Johnny St Cyr on banjo, Johnny Dodds on clarinet and alto sax, Kid Ory on trombone, and Lil Hardin and Armstrong on piano. At first, the band adhered to the collective New Orleans style, but as the recordings progressed Armstrong emerged as a virtuoso soloist. He began to develop as a singer as well, his voice conjuring unpredictably with the beat. The Hot Fives, and later Hot Sevens (with tuba and drums) brought jazz to the fore as a music for listening, as well as an incidental music for leisure.

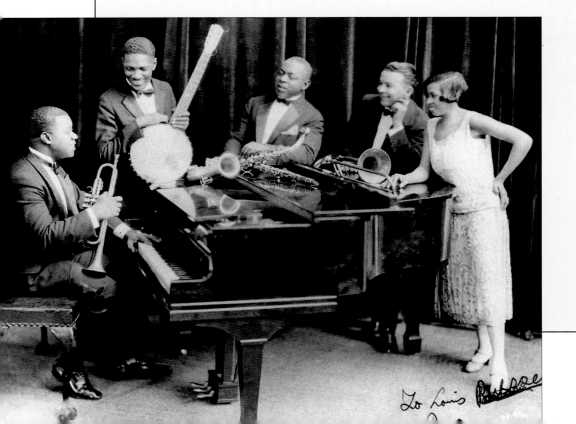

The great Louis Armstrong Hot Five with (from left) Armstrong seated at the piano, Johnny St Cyr on banjo, Johnny Dodds on clarinet, Kid Ory on trombone, and pianist Lil Hardin standing, right. The Hot Five was the greatest of the early small jazz bands.

Trumpeter Miles Davis was a genius as a player, but a genius as a chooser of musicians, too. Listeners way beyond the jazz cognoscenti heard the 1959 album 'Kind of Blue', which marked the rising influence of the modal over the chord-based improvising style of bebop, and the sound of Davis (centre) with Cannonball Adderley (left), bassist Paul Chambers (second from left) and John Coltrane (right). This is Newport, 1958.

Charlie Parker Quintet

In the early 1940s many informal and rapidly changing ensembles sprang out of the late-night sessions at Minton's playhouse in Harlem from which the new style of bebop emerged. But it was a Charlie Parker quintet featuring trumpeter Dizzy Gillespie that brought this new music to a spectacular high point. His music was not recorded because of the American Federation of Musicians' recording strike from 1942, but his work as a leader in 1945 and 1946 produced some of the most breathtaking recordings since Armstrong's Hot Fives and Sevens.

In 1945 Parker and Gillespie regularly worked together in chamber-sized groups, a relationship that survived until the following year, when heroin and alcohol dependency caused Parker to be committed to a mental hospital. On his release, he formed a new quintet with his young disciple Miles Davis, pianist Duke Jorden, bassist Tommy Potter, and drummer Max Roach – and though Davis did not have Gillespie's dazzling agility, in some respects the band was Parker's most empathetic ensemble. Using a repertoire of souped-up blues progressions and standard pop songs adapted to make the improvisation more demanding (and to avoid paying royalties on the originals), the band displayed breathtaking ingenuity and the rhythm section's work was intimately interwoven with the front line, rather than simply accompanying it.

Miles Davis Group

For a man of legendary ego, Miles Davis led some of the most collectively minded ensembles in jazz. His playing constantly complemented the work of his partners, and his 'comeback' band in the mid 1950s displayed astonishing collective alertness. The acoustic groups that followed, from the late 1950s to the mid-1960s, further merged the complex extended solo approach of the post-war period with an ensemble energy that recalled the earliest jazz.

Davis used a nucleus of players from his late-1950s groups (alternating pianist Bill Evans with the more regular Wynton Kelly), with boppish alto saxophonist Julian 'Cannonball' Adderly partnering John Coltrane on tenor. For this more relaxed music, Davis chose a less attacking drummer, Jimmy Cobb. By his choice of players and repertoire, he allowed the soloists to improvise more reflectively. The trumpeter intensified his small-group music in 1963, with Wayne Short, pianist Herbie Hancock, bassist Ron Carter and drummer Tony Williams – yet even at full throttle, this band still played as if it could hear a pin drop.

with 60,000 or 70,000 copies in the first year. It became his signature. I don't know how Coltrane felt about playing it every night, but I remember sitting on a bus in Japan and somebody pulled out a European tape of "My Favourite Things" from, maybe, two and a half years later, and it was still just so astonishingly inventive. It was just a miracle what he could do on a nightly basis.

'I think that the symbolic and the real moment where he really divides his audience in two, and divides jazz in two and forever, and alters its sensibility, is in November 1961 when he goes to the Village Vanguard. Now you have to remember, that a year earlier he had "My Favourite Things" out, an unlikely hit, played on the radio all the time, made him a big *bona fide* jazz celebrity. So he goes to the Vanguard in November and everybody's expecting to hear "My Favourite Things", which of course he played. But it's at that engagement that he produces his 15-minute blues yelp, "Chasin' The Trane", which was a completely unprecedented sustained howl, to use Alan Ginsberg's word, that completely sundered the audience.'

Coltrane's later bands were controversial,
even with the musicians who played in them.
With Pharoah Sanders (centre, on tenor),
bassist Jimmy Garrison and drummer Rashied
Ali, Coltrane began to develop a looser,
wilder music.

The evidence on Coltrane's classic recordings leaps from
the speakers. In 1997 Impulse Records released a reissue
of a luxurious series of classic sessions – the Village
Vanguard live recordings of 1961, cut not long after
Coltrane left the Miles Davis band.

They featured improvisation of a beauty and sustained
force rarely heard from Coltrane before that winter, and
musicians still marvel at their freshness. These November
1961 dates are widely regarded as Coltrane's rite of
passage, as he left the relatively secure harmonic world of
bebop's chord-structures and stepped into inner space.
The opening notes of 'Chasin' The Trane' sound like the
terse and gritty hard bop lines that were the
saxophonist's trademark in the 1950s, but resolutions
are left hanging, expressed in fractured pitch, or intoned
like Middle Eastern music; the swing is bumpier and
darker; Coltrane's phrasing is more fragmentary and
episodic, like a kind of urgent, high-pitched praying, and
there often seems to be more than one line active in his
solo. Gary Giddins, the *Village Voice*'s respected jazz
critic, remembers the reactions:

'The old Coltrane fans were offended, and the reviews
were just scathing – *Downbeat* called it one big air leak,
referred to him as anti-jazz, musical nonsense, those
kinds of phrases, boring, monotonous . . . but a whole
other group of younger listeners, my generation and
even the one before, we were just inflamed by it. Boy, it
really caught our imagination, it had so much
excitement to it – you know, where's it going to go? It
was like 80 choruses that performance, an absolutely
thrilling thing. And it just changed the whole music,
hundreds of young musicians round the country heard
that, and records like it that Coltrane made, and became
excited about jazz in a way that they hadn't been before.'

The Village Vanguard recordings reveal not just a
seachange in Coltrane's own playing, but the coalescing
of an inner circle of musicians dedicated to his own
vision. During 1960 and 1961 he had experimented with
a variety of partners, including the young pianist McCoy
Tyner (a fellow-Philadelphian and family friend),
Ornette Coleman's fizzing, light-touch drummer
Billy Higgins, classical-trained percussionist Pete LaRoca
and the earthier, most Africanised drummer of all of
them, Elvin Jones, one of a celebrated jazz dynasty of
Joneses that included pianist Hank and trumpeter Thad.
The saxophonist's groups even briefly included the
guitarist Wes Montgomery, a musician that Coltrane
probably sensed was as intuitive as himself, but who he

The great pianist McCoy Tyner. Tyner
was central to Coltrane's conception
from the early to middle 1960s, and his
stormy, chord-heavy playing perfectly
complemented the leader, although he
didn't agree with Coltrane's later
experiments.

With McCoy Tyner's departure, John Coltrane's last bands featured his pianist wife, Alice. A player of sparer technique but a resourceful conjuror of atmosphere, she often used organ as well as piano.

discovered was for the most part contented with the lilt of the popular song. The adventurous saxophonist and bass clarinettist Eric Dolphy, a man who combined Charlie Parker's legato fluency with startling leaps across the registers, became a frequent guest and a significant contributor to the group. However, it was Jones and Tyner who were the best creators of the counterbalancing tensions that Coltrane needed to be pulled between, and with the arrival of bassist Jimmy Garrison, a Philadelphia musician with all the skills the leader needed from bop-walks, to raga-drones, to free-improvising openness, one of the most creative jazz ensembles of all time was complete.

John Coltrane was, of course, inhabiting a real world of commercial imperatives at the same time. Committed as producer Bob Thiele's adventurous Impulse label was to sustaining, literally, Coltrane's impulses (as well as several other of the black 'New Thing' musicians who

were exploring looser and more free-associative forms of jazz at the time), it also had to pay the rent. That pragmatism invited a positive disposition towards show tunes and romantic ballad playing that, until his last years, Coltrane didn't mind, and also led to collaborations with jazz celebrities – including Duke Ellington, who he recorded a delicate ballad session with in 1962, featuring the exquisite 'In A Sentimental Mood'.

This was a tumultuous period of the saxophonist's life. His marriage to Naima capsized, but Coltrane met a new life-partner who became a musical partner as well. She bore the name of his mother, and sustained the connection even as far as playing the piano. Alice McLeod, a former student of Bud Powell's, had been pianist with the vibraharpist Terry Gibbs and met Coltrane on tour. They had a son, John Jnr, in 1964. In that year the band also recorded one of the most sombre and melancholy, but exquisitely textured Coltrane albums, *Crescent*. Ed Jones hails it as:

'As the 1950s closed, John Coltrane was still suspended between two worlds.'

'. . . one of Coltrane's highest artistic moments – all sax players talk about that amazing sound that he got, a full, rounded, singing, beautiful clear tone.'

In December, partly inspired by the birth of his child, Coltrane recorded one of his most triumphant achievements. 'A Love Supreme' was a four-part devotional work that featured one of the wildest and most elemental displays of polyrhythmic drumming ever heard from Elvin Jones, and a mantra-like repeating theme – beginning with a four-note pattern from Jimmy Garrison's bass. This theme was echoed, in a call-and-response fashion by the horn. It modulated through several keys, and turned, hypnotically, into a guttural vocal chant performed by all four players, as if they had succeded in reducing the music to its simplest essence.

With his pacifism, non-western spiritual sympathies, anti-materialism and apparent indifference to record-industry pressures, Coltrane was a fitting symbol for a generation that was mistrustful of capitalist consumerism. Explicit civil rights messages can be heard in his music now – 'Psalm', the majestically poignant conclusion of 'A Love Supreme' echoes the previous year's 'Alabama', which was inspired by a Martin Luther King speech, and a bombing atrocity that killed four black schoolchildren. Jazz historian James Lincoln Collier believes that John Coltrane's jazz sainthood was partly down to these instinctive alliances, and partly to happenstance:

'Coltrane benefited from the Woodstock attitude. "A Love Supreme" and "My Favourite Things" both begin with very simple melodies, very simple understandable kinds of music, and then as they begin to sweep along and become more abstract, he's drawing his audience in as he goes. But you had an audience there that was prepared philosophically for something different.'

Evan Parker describes Coltrane's beliefs:

'He was a very spiritual man, religious, but interested in a kind of world ecumenical version of religion, looking for what Islam, Hinduism, Christianity have in common, rather than staying within the religious background that he was raised in. So there was a kind of universality about his approach which touched a lot of people.'

Coltrane with the soprano saxophone in his heyday of the mid-1960s. Apart from Sidney Bechet and Steve Lacy, Coltrane was almost alone in using this difficult, high-pitched instrument. But after he adopted it in 1960, saxophonists everywhere took it up.

In its celebration of blues, church music and vocalised folk idioms 'A Love Supreme' triumphantly celebrated the black American experience, and its links to Africa. Drummer Elvin Jones gives one of the performances of his life, a *tour de force* of overlaid rhythmic patterns and almost superhuman complexity. But the quartet was already experiencing pressures from inside and out.

Coltrane himself was proceeding by a mixture of inner vision and outward creative pragmatism. He was convinced that there was more beyond even the quartet that had liberated him, but he also drew together younger players whose sounds he liked, just to see what would happen. Coltrane's continuing restlessness began to irritate, first McCoy Tyner and then Elvin Jones. A mid-1965 session using a greatly augmented

'You could use this record ('Ascension') to heat your apartment on those cold winter days.' MARION BROWN

band performed the collective improvisation 'Ascension'. Owing something to the approach of the eccentric Chicago avant-garde bandleader Sun Ra's unique brand of abstract vaudeville, and the techniques of Ra's tenor player John Gilmore, 'Ascension' also harked back to revolutionary saxophonist Ornette Coleman's *Free Jazz* album of five years earlier, particularly in the bold use of a spontaneously interactive double-quartet augmenting his regular one.

'Ascension' shifted between hoarse collective roars of sound, exclamatory staccato exchanges and voices emerging from the tumult, sometimes alone and sometimes in whirling conversation, and then falling back. Although often exhibiting rather dissonant tonality, the piece still gave off an astonishingly warm glow. A participant on the session, saxophonist Marion Brown said, 'You could use this record to heat your apartment on those cold winter days.' The session

became a model for the larger free-jazz groups of the 1960s and 1970s, and was one of John Coltrane's most ambitious and lasting contributions to postwar jazz.

Coltrane was both creating and gravitating towards a new kind of jazz improviser. His own disciples were moving even further out. He described Pharoah Sanders, a saxophonist on 'Ascension' who had virtually abandoned scales entirely in favour of sustained, braying hollers, as a 'huge spiritual reservoir'. A growing number of newcomers appeared on open-house sessions, which led Bob Thiele, the Impulse producer, to observe that if he had signed everybody that Coltrane recommended during that time 'we'd have 400 musicians on the label'. One such musician was drummer Rashied Ali, an Elvin Jones disciple almost ten years Coltrane's junior and who shared much of his background (Philadelphia, the Granoff School and rhythm-and-blues). He was dispersing the 'beat' into an ebb-and-flow of sound even more ambiguous than that of his model, shifting the contribution of the drummer ever more towards shading and texture and away from layers and recombinations of repeating patterns. As Coltrane moved closer to pure sound, Ali was his logical shadow.

Tyner, and then Jones, left the band (the former to be replaced by Alice McLeod) in 1965, the year that the couple also had a second child, named Ravi after Ravi Shankar. Pharoah Sanders also joined the band as a second saxophonist, and John Coltrane's music finally moved to a fearsomely abstract point that many jazz fans could barely recognise as rooted in the music's traditions (particularly his starting point of bebop) at all. In 1966 John and Alice were married, and a third son, Oran was born, but the saxophonist was in increasing abdominal pain, and his remarkable strength was failing him.

Five months before his death from liver disease at 40 however, he made one of his finest recordings, entirely on the tenor sax and purely in duo conversation with Rashied Ali. The ensemble simplicity of *Interstellar Space* seems close to the very tranquillity and fluidity of line for which he was searching. It was as if John Coltrane needed to absorb, exhaust and abandon not only the mixed European and African-American structural principles of the music he had inherited to find his voice, but also the most fundamental attributes of the jazz band as well. Countless exploratory musicians since have devoted themselves to the pursuit of just where Coltrane's dream might have gone had he lived. *Village Voice* critic Gary Giddins explains:

'Coltrane was a very important figure, not only musically but culturally. The rest of the world may have been obsessed with The Beatles and Bob Dylan at the time, but there were a lot of people especially in the United States for whom Coltrane was our voice, and we followed him to see where he was going to go. The avant-garde itself, yes, it depleted the jazz audience because it was too difficult – it was in a way a kind of post-modernist music, which means that in order to really understand it you have to understand everything that came before it, so if you were a jazz enthusiast and you were excited by the tradition itself, and how it got from Louis Armstrong and Duke Ellington to Charlie Parker and Dizzy Gillespie, to Miles and Thelonious Monk to Ornette Coleman and Coltrane, then you could see what he was responding to, and that was a thrilling thing. But if you didn t know, and you just walked into it blank, then you heard what could just seem like a lot of hollering.

'I think the progression of art is always to question the conventions we accept – why we accept them, and what will happen if we don't. I mean if people tell you for hundreds or even thousands of years that music should be ordered by bar lines and measures, somebody eventually is going to say, "Hey, what happens if I kick away all the bar lines?" And then you have Cecil Taylor and Ornette Coleman. If somebody says, "Oh, you've got to play chord changes", somebody's going to say, "Well, what happens if I replace the chord changes with scales?" Like George Russell and Miles Davis and Bill Evans and Coltrane. If somebody tells you that you've got to play four-four all the time, somebody's going to say, "Well, wait a second, we can have a jazz-waltz, we can play in six, we can play in eight, we can play in eleven, we can play in five", and somebody's finally going to say, "Hey, what if we kick off time altogether, and play a kind of one-one where the beat is completely free?"

'He didn't intend to leave a gap – he intended that there be more space for everybody to do what they should do.'

Then we're going to have a free, fortuitous kind of harmony, melody's going to be the centre of the music and whatever harmony arises will be serendipitous, a consequence of the melody we play – and that's the exact opposite of the jazz tradition, which begins with a harmony you invent, and then a melody that goes with the harmony.

'So all of these questions are almost inevitable, and the issue is not only, are you going to have the nerve to ask them and act on them, but do you have the genius to bring it off? And Coltrane surely did, and Coleman and Taylor, and a handful of others did, and that's why their music is going to live and it has lived. The geniuses are always the ones who are a step ahead of us and we eventually catch up. Thelonious Monk said it very well many years ago. He said, "Don't play like they tell you to play, you play like you want, and 15, 20 years later they'll catch up".'

Discography

In recent years there has been a flood of re-issues of what is now called 'classic jazz', and for those new to the music there is too much to choose from. We have attempted to list a handful of major works by our six Heroes. Catalogue details will vary from country to country, and new issues will make the material available in different combinations from time to time, as boxed-set collections in this area increase in popularity – but the recording dates and original titles will give most dealers an idea of what you are looking for.

Dizzy Gillespie

The Complete RCA Victor Recordings (RCA/Bluebird)
RECORDING DATES: 1937-1949
RCA recordings by Gillespie from the middle to late 1940s, plus some early material featuring him with the Teddy Hill Band. Classics like 'Night in Tunisia' and 'Manteca' are there, the pioneering bop big band with Chano Pozo on congas gets a good airing, and there's some attractive post-Parker bebop with the great Don Byas on saxophone. Gillespie's trumpet sounds typically bristling and urgent, and the recording quality is good for the era.
Personnel includes: JJ Johnson, James Moody, Don Byas, Milt Jackson, Kenny Clarke, Chano Pozo, Lionel Hampton.

The Charlie Parker Story (Denon/Savoy)
RECORDING DATES: 1945
Not issued under Dizzy's name, but intriguingly featuring him on both piano and trumpet in the cutting-edge bebop band that virtually put the whole story on the map. Ownership of this essential Savoy material has changed hands a good deal over the years, but it is always available in some form. Frequently shambolic recording sessions nevertheless produced explosive music, turning points in postwar jazz, including 'Billie's Bounce', 'Now's the Time' and 'Ko-Ko', and 'Thriving From a Riff' (based on the 'I Got Rhythm' chord sequence) is a good demonstration of the bebop appropriation method. Gillespie only plays trumpet on 'Ko-Ko' here (but his solos on it are astonishing reminders of his harmonic sophistication), but a good deal of apposite piano.
Personnel includes: Dizzy Gillespie, Miles Davis, Max Roach.

Diz and Getz (Verve)
RECORDING DATES: 1953-1954
From the brief period of Gillespie's guest spot with the Stan Kenton band, and a fine example of the still developing poise and control of his technique. The music isn't as ferocious and headlong as the bop breakthroughs of a decade before, but the newly-discovered Oscar Peterson's trio does a pretty efficient job, Getz (as he often did in those days) sounds grittily cool rather than evaporating-cool, and there's some Gillespie conga playing here and there.
Personnel includes: Stan Getz, Oscar Peterson, Max Roach.

Pleyel Concert 1953 (Vogue)
RECORDING DATE: 1953
Gillespie began to recombine his early experiences in the swing bands with the insights of bop during the early 1950s, with the result that his music became more accessible and his solo playing more amiably imperious. On this set from Paris, Gillespie rolls through a mixed bebop and vaudeville repertoire with a relatively unexceptional group, but his own playing is magnificent.
Personnel includes: Wade Legge, Al Jones.

Max & Dizzy 1989 (A&M)
RECORDING DATE: 1989
Co-founders of bebop in captivating communion in Paris in 1989. Gillespie was paired with Max Roach for this historic encounter, and both men perform as if the years that had passed since they first forged bop were as nothing.
Personnel includes: Dizzy Gillespie, Max Roach.

Thelonious Monk

Complete Blue Note Recordings (Blue Note)
RECORDING DATES: 1947-1958

Thelonious Monk's Blue Note sessions of the late 1940s and early 1950s resulted in some of the most compelling jazz music ever recorded. Compositions such as 'Straight No Chaser'. 'Well You Needn't' and 'Round Midnight' indicate how independently his conception navigated the jazz world around him, and the solo piano passages reveal a much more complex deconstructed virtuoso than the man who simply left long pauses between clanking chords. Some of the recording and the certainty of the bands about where they're headed is dubious, but the partnership with vibraharpist Milt Jackson is fascinating – and even the live material from the famous Five Spot sessions of 1957, recorded on John Coltrane's tape recorder, is interesting, if hovering on the edge of audio acceptability.

Personnel includes: Kenny Dorham, Sonny Rollins, John Coltrane, Art Blakey, Max Roach, Roy Haynes.

Brilliant Corners (Original Jazz Classics)
RECORDING DATE: 1956

A session with Sonny Rollins and Max Roach, and one of Monk's finest outings of the 1950s, signalling his shift to Riverside Records under the wing of Orrin Keepnews. The music challenged the players so much that the final issue of the title tune was stitched together from a variety of takes, but classic tracks include 'Pannonica', 'Bernsha Swing', 'Ba-lue Bolivar Ba-lues Are' and 'I Surrender Dear'.

Personnel includes: Sonny Rollins, Max Roach, Clark Terry.

Misterioso (Original Jazz Classics)
RECORDING DATE: 1958

Live recording of the 1958 Monk band that featured tenorist Johnny Griffin, with Ahmed Abdul Malik on bass and Roy Haynes on drums. Griffin was less inclined to take much notice of Monk's lopsided signposts than most sidemen, and his quicksilver bebop style allows him to hurtle through the repertoire as if he'd written it himself. Griffin's excitement is a good counterbalance for Monk, and drummer Roy Haynes is as tastefully urgent as ever.

Personnel includes: John Griffin, Roy Haynes.

Alone in San Francisco (Original Jazz Classics)
RECORDING DATE: 1959

One of the best routes to understanding the quirky mechanics of Monk's unique piano style. This is Monk unaccompanied, and it's a masterly performance, more reflective and introverted but superb in dynamic control. He doggedly dismantles the structures of his materials and rebuilds them in his own way. His famous 'Blue Monk' is on this recording as well as five other originals but he also turns his formidable attention to some standard songs, including 'There's Danger in Your Eyes' and 'Cherie'.

Personnel includes: Thelonious Monk.

It's Monk's Time (Columbia)
RECORDING DATE: 1964

By this stage in his career, Monk was beginning to be widely accepted (1964 was the year his face got on the cover of **Time** magazine) and inevitably his concerts became a repetition of the great compositions of earlier years. His treatment of them remains fresh however, and this band, with the understated saxophonist Charlie Rouse, was one of the most appropriate of the later period. The spiky 'Shuffle Boil' is one of the outstanding features of this session.

Personnel includes: Charles Rouse, Butch Warren, Ben Riley.

Gerry Mulligan

The Best of the Gerry Mulligan Quartet with Chet Baker (Pacific Jazz)
RECORDING DATES: 1952-1957

The sound that defined Cool Jazz for a wider and younger audience in the 1950s. Mulligan heard jazz as intertwining lines rather than endless improvisers' monologues, and he disliked groups that he felt that had to shout to get an effect as well. Chet Baker, although not as theoretically literate and adventurous as Mulligan, had virtually the perfect trumpet tone for this kind of reserved contrapuntal music, and the blending of the two musicians in this classic band is one of the triumphant relationships of jazz. This set covers their albums from 1952 and 1953, with their 1957 reunion also referred to. The mood is warm, the music conversational, and the tracks include the famous 'Walking Shoes' and Baker's timeless hit with 'My Funny Valentine'.

Personnel includes: Chet Baker, Chico Hamilton, Dave Bailey.

At Storyville (Pacific Jazz)
RECORDING DATES: 1956

More clever and intricate multi-threaded jazz from a Mulligan 1950s band, but this time with the valve trombonist Bob Brookmeyer doing a pretty creditable job of substituting for the disgruntled and departed Chet Baker. Brookmeyer doesn't quite have the seat-of-the-pants reflexes and lazy romanticism of Baker, but the valve trombone is trumpet-like, and he meshes into the general idea as if it were made for it. The ensemble writing and the background fills have all of Mulligan's usual light and classy precision, both he and Brookmeyer shift to piano when it's appropriate, and the whole set is almost as much of a musicianly delight as its better-known predecessor.

Personnel includes: Bob Brookmeyer, Bill Crow, Dave Bailey.

Blues In Time (Verve)
RECORDING DATES: 1957

Underestimated but very interesting variation on the classic Mulligan-Baker pianoless set up, mainly because it features a modest but deliciously delicate artist of the Cool manner in alto saxophonist Paul Desmond – more usually heard with the famous Dave Brubeck, but usually better in other contexts. Desmond had a tone like bone china, a hypnotic way of phrasing behind the beat, and his melodic imagination was rich and unclinched, as can be heard on a version of 'Body and Soul'. Mulligan, as if equally fascinated, takes a back seat role in much of this session.

Personnel includes: Paul Desmond, Joe Benjamin, Dave Bailey.

Age of Steam (A&M)
RECORDING DATES: 1971

Mulligan's effective combination of relaxed swing, dynamic evenness and graceful harmonic mobility, at work on a set of pieces devoted to the leader's enthusiasm for steam railways, and bearing appropriate titles. It's a makeover for some excellent material he wrote for the 14-piece Concert Band in the early 1970s and features an excellent outfit of sympathetic partners including trombonist Bob Brookmeyer and trumpeter Harry Edison.

Personnel includes: Harry 'Sweets' Edison, Bob Brookmeyer, Bud Shank.

Rebirth of the Cool (GRP)
RECORDING DATES: 1992

A remake of the Birth of the Cool sessions of 1948, originally intended for Miles Davis, substituting his young admirer Wallace Roney after Davis' death in 1991. Mulligan and pianist Lohn Lewis were original participants, and not surprisingly the session is much better than first time around. Mulligan plays superbly, and Phil Woods' recreation of the sustained alto note (first delivered by the young Lee Konitz) over the floating harmonic movement of 'Moon Dreams' is still magic.

Personnel includes: Wallace Roney, Phil Woods, John Lewis.

Ella Fitzgerald

The Original Decca Recording (GRP/Decca)
RECORDING DATES: 1938-1955

As part of the 75th birthday tributes to Ella Fitzgerald in 1993, GRP assembled this book-format package with 39 tracks covering the period from 1938 to 1955. The hit that made her name, 'A-Tisket-A-Tasket', is there, the Chick Webb band on 'Undecided', and various performances with the Ink Spots and the Delta Rhythm Boys. It is interesting to see how quickly the basic Fitzgerald method has slotted into place – the control of intonation and manipulation of the beat, the transparent, deceptively artless delivery, the furious swing. Fitzgerald's scat technique gets the full works on 'Oh Lady Be Good', and her trumpet-like accompaniment of Louis Armstrong's singing on 'Dream a Little Dream of Me' is delightful. One of her most suitable piano partnerships, with Ellis Larkins, is also well represented on such tracks as 'Until the Real Thing Comes Along'.
Personnel includes: Chick Webb, Louis Jordan, The Ink Spots, Ray Brown.

The Best of the Songbooks (Verve)
RECORDING DATES: 1956-1964

Fitzgerald's recordings for Norman Granz's Verve label, and the mould-breaking move towards the Songbook's series, are hard to filter down to a compilation. But even in truncated form it is easy to hear how the singer's performances so successfully matched the qualities of the original material. This is the set for lovers of the great tradition of American popular song and show-tune writing. Granz had his eye on a much wider audience for Ella Fitzgerald, and 16 of the Songbook tracks are included here, including 'Ev'ry Time We Say Goodbye', and 'Bewitched, Bothered and Bewildered'.
Personnel includes: Ben Webster, Stuff Smith, Barney Kessel.

The Complete Songbooks (Verve)
RECORDING DATES: 1956-1964

This is the major commitment if you find yourself a besotted Ella fan and you win the lottery or know somebody who has. This 18-CD set covers the whole works, from the highly successful Cole Porter exercise of 1956 that set the whole show in motion, through the magnificent Gershwin project, and the slightly unsteady partnership with Duke Ellington's orchestra that nevertheless results in a fascinating balance between Fitzgerald's pin-sharp accuracy and the band's elemental surges.
Personnel includes: As above.

Ella and Basie (Verve)
Recording dates: 1963

Lively and vigorous partnership between Ella and the Count Basie Orchestra – the latter was legendary for swinging as hard as she does, and its more direct approach and explosive ensemble sound suits Fitzgerald well.
Personnel includes: Joe Newman, Frank Foster, Count Basie.

Mack the Knife – The Complete Ella in Berlin (Verve)
Recording dates: 1960

Apart from the Songbooks, this was some of Ella Fitzgerald's best-known work. Live recording gives a powerful flavour of how charismatic she could be in concert in her prime, and she applies breathtaking technical surgery masked by bouyant exuberance to classics like 'Lady is A Tramp', 'The Man I Love' and 'Just One of Those Things'. The idea that Ella Fitzgerald was too modest and shy, even in her prime, to be a relaxed and witty entertainer is also laid to rest here, and a freewheeling humour underpins much of the interpretation.
Personnel includes: Jim Hall, Barney Kessel.

Wes Montgomery

Far Wes (Pacific)
RECORDING DATES: 1958-1959

The years of Montgomery's oddly-paced career when he believed he was playing better than he was ever to do later on. The guitarist's huge strengths – his tone, his improvising freshness, his fluency and eager swing – all are evident, although the situations he was apt to function in were sometimes a little on the soporific side. The trustworthy, if generally undistinguished skills of brother Monk on bass and Buddy on piano keep the session moving, but the other solo star is really Harold Land on tenor, a superb and largely overlooked artist with a delectably dry, reserved approach. Leila includes some of Montgomery's most explicit tributes to Django Reinhardt.

Personnel includes: Pony Poindexter, Harold Land, Buddy Montgomery , Monk Montgomery.

Incredible Jazz Guitar (Original Jazz Classics)
RECORDING DATES: 1960

If you bought no other Wes Montgomery record, this would be the one to go for. It was always the most forthright and relaxed of his studio sessions, not least because a brilliant rhythm section (Tommy Flanagan on piano, Percy Heath and Albert Heath on bass and drums) keeps it boiling throughout, and although the guitarist's weaknesses for rather insubstantial tunes blunts the impact of the later tracks, the headlong bebop of Sonny Rollins' 'Airegin' and Montgomery's walking-bassline theme tune 'Four on Six' finds Montgomery in unquenchable form, with all of his formidable technical equipment unfurled.

Personnel includes: Tommy Flanagan, Percy Heath, Albert Heath.

Full House (Original Jazz Classics)
RECORDING DATES: 1962

There aren't many opportunities to hear Wes Montgomery, a guitarist with a sax-like technique, jamming with a saxophonist his absolute equal for speed of thought, imagination and exuberance. This is one of the best, and best-known.

Montgomery's partnership with Johnny 'Little Giant' Griffin, a man who was famous in the bebop business for hurtling through chord changes as if the fastest tempos were a stroll. The disc came after Montgomery's move towards easy-listening had begun, so it was telling proof that the Creed Taylor experience no more blunted his deepest instincts than it did for George Benson.

Personnel includes: Johnny Griffin, Wynton Kelly, Paul Chambers, Jimmy Cobb.

The Verve Jazz Sides (Verve)
Recording dates: 1964-66

Not a bad compilation of the most controversial and, for the most part, disappointing phase of Wes Montgomery's briefly brilliant career. The arrangements of Wes' virtual signature tune, 'West Coast Blues', and an uptempo account of Duke Ellington and Juan Tizol's 'Caravan' are pretty yawn-inducing, but the Jimmy Smith collaborations do crank up the heartrate and the decibels. Best thing on the set, however is the music from the famous *Smokin' At the Half Note* session, with pianist Wynton Kelly. This probably captures the sound of Wes Montgomery cutting loose in a club more effectively than almost anything he recorded, and is well worth having – even at the price of a good deal of the rest.

Personnel includes: Jimmy Smith, Wynton Kelly, Ray Barretto, Jimmy Cobb.

John Coltrane

Kind of Blue (Columbia/Sony)
RECORDING DATES: 1959
A disc issued under Miles Davis' name, of course, and one of his most famous – but fascinating also as a showcase for the sound of John Coltrane, and an indication of his movement away from chords and towards modal playing around this time. The music is absolutely taut and focussed throughout , and is both a jazz landmark and a journey through key landmarks for Coltrane himself.
Personnel includes: Miles Davis, Bill Evans, Cannonball Adderley, Wynton Kelly.

Giant Steps (Atlantic)
RECORDING DATES: 1959
The end of chord-change playing, as far as Coltrane was concerned. As saxophonist Evan Parker says, the title track sounds like a learned exercise that Coltrane was playing to make a point – delivering arpeggios faster, and with more transformations than ever before, just to show the time had come to call it a day.
Personnel includes: Tommy Flanagan, Paul Chambers, Art Taylor.

Africa Brass 1&2 (MCA)
RECORDING DATES: 1961
A 1961 performance by a Coltrane group expanded to 14 pieces, including the restlessly experimental reed player Eric Dolphy. Dolphy did much of the preparation for this telling session, and Coltrane's own playing is often staggering. The track that stands out is 'Africa', but there's early warning of the saxophonist's move to soprano on the improbable but trenchantly interpreted 'Greensleeves'.
Personnel includes: Freddie Hubbard, Eric Dolphy, Pat Patrick, Booker Little, McCoy Tyner, Elvin Jones.

The Complete Live at The Village Vanguard (GRP/Impulse)
RECORDING DATES: 1961
Recently reworked set now taking in all four nights of this memorable engagement, the one that, as Gary Giddins puts it, 'competely sundered' Coltrane's audience. 'Chasin' the Trane', with its protracted, howling, free-jazz solo indicates how comprehensively Coltrane had broken with the lyrical arpeggiated style that produced 'My Favourite Things'.
Personnel includes: Eric Dolphy, McCoy Tyner, Reggie Workman, Elvin Jones.

A Love Supreme (MCA)
RECORDING DATES: 1964
Probably Coltrane's best-known session. This is a four-part devotional work featuring the most focussed and resolved Coltrane band, and Elvin Jones' drumming is a breathtaking display of polyrhythmic playing that washes over the others but bears them up into space at the same time.
Personnel includes: McCoy Tyner, Jimmy Garrison, Elvin Jones.

The Major Works of John Coltrane (GRP/Impulse)
RECORDING DATES: 1965
This two-disc set includes two versions of 'Ascension', Coltrane's angle of Ornette Coleman's earlier Free Jazz experiment for loose improvisation in flexible structures within larger bands, and a beacon for bigger free-jazz groups ever after.
Personnel includes: McCoy Tyner, Jimmy Garrison, Elvin Jones, Eric Dolphy, Freddie Hubbard, Pharoah Saunders.

Interstellar Space (GRP/Impulse)
RECORDING DATES: 1967
One of the last, an atmospheric duet recording for Coltrane with the unpredictable, texture-orientated drummer Rashied-Ali. With a softer context and less competition, Coltrane's vocabulary is all the more audible, and his understanding with Ali – so controversial to his earlier fans – is clear. An indication of where things might have gone.
Personnel includes: Rashied Ali.

Index

Page numbers in *italics* refer to illustrations.
Page numbers in **bold** refer to main entries.

PHOTO CREDITS

Photographs on the following pages are reproduced by kind permission:

ARBITER pages 30,69 & 112
CORBIS-BETTMAN pages 8,11, 12, 32, 51, 88 & 91; UPI pages 15, 31, 78, 79 & 97.
FRANK DRIGGS COLLECTION pages 34, 42, 70 & 120; Joe Alper page 119.
GETTY IMAGES pages 96 & 105
IMAGE BANK/ARCHIVE PHOTOS pages 89 & 116; Frank Driggs Collection page 83; Metronome pages 68 & 74.
JAZZ INDEX: Christian Him pages 66-7, 85 & 144; C. Huggins page 1; Max Jones pages 18, 21, 92 & 115; Peter Vacher pages 33, 73, 135 & 137 (Courtesy Mainline Picture Release): Peter Vacher Collection/Ernie Garside page 133; F.Winham page 142.
MAX JONES ARCHIVE page 49.
MAGNUM: Frank Driggs Collection pages 86-7, 93, 101 & 141: Wayne Miller page 99, Guy Le Querrec pages 22, 23, 24, 40, 60, 64, 65 & 130; W. Eugene Smith pages 46-7; Dennis Stock pages 17, 37 & 81.
REDFERN'S: William Gottlieb pages 6-7 left, 16, 19, 28, 29, 35, 48, 52, 57, 102, 109 & 131; Max Jones Archive pages 9, 56, 94, 100, 140 & 145; Max Jones Archive/Bob Parelt page 58; Michael Ochs Archives pages 2, 7 right, 61 & 77; David Redfern pages 26-7, 45, 62, 106-7, 108, 111, 117, 125, 126-7, 139 & 143; Chuck Stewart pages 59, 128 & 132.
DUNCAN SCHIEDT pages 39.
UDEN ASSOCIATES Pages 118 & 123

Jacket images:
CORBIS-BETTMAN/UPI: Gerry Mulligan, Dizzy Gillespie, John Coltrane
JAZZ INDEX: Mick Doyle: Thelonious Monk,
JAZZ INDEX: Max Jones: Ella Fitzgerald,
JAZZ INDEX: F. Winham:Wes Montgomery

ACKNOWLEDGEMENTS

As ever, the most useful catch-all in this delicate circumstance is the enlightened British teacher and jazz philosopher Conrad Cork's open-handed acknowledgement 'I owe everything to everybody'. But in particular, and first and foremost, I owe the usual heartfelt thanks at book-time to my family – to Ros, Fred and Leo. Thanks are also due to the *Guardian* newspaper, which has been my jazz guardian for the past 20 years. Special thanks to Nick, Janice, Jo, Luca and Melissa at Uden Associates, among essential others, who made the *Jazz Heroes* TV series for British television's Channel 4, and to Patrick Uden who shot the idea into the air in the first place. Astonished thanks to Sarah and Corinne at Collins & Brown, who rode with every prevarication. Thanks also to Steve Engelhard and Neville Young for nifty disk work. And extra special thanks to all those musicians, critics and music-lovers who contributed to the series and to this book. They are the witnesses to one of the most remarkable musical phenomena of modern times, and their testimony tells it as it is.